D0203694

Kenneth Grahame

Twayne's English Authors Series

Kinley E. Roby, Editor

Northeastern University

TEAS 449

KENNETH GRAHAME
(1859–1932)
Reproduced by permission of the
Bodleian Library, Oxford, England.

Kenneth Grahame

By Lois R. Kuznets

San Diego State University

Twayne Publishers
A Division of G.K. Hall & Co. • Boston

Kenneth Grahame

Lois R. Kuznets

Copyright 1987 by G.K. Hall & Co.
All Rights Reserved
Published by Twayne Publishers
A Division of G.K. Hall & Co.
70 Lincoln Street
Boston, Massachusetts 02111

Copyediting supervised by Lewis DeSimone
Book design by Barbara Anderson

Typeset in 11 pt. Garamond
by P&M Typesetting, Waterbury, Connecticut

Printed on permanent/durable acid-free paper
and bound in the United States of America

Library of Congress Cataloging in Publication Data

Kuznets, Lois R.
  Kenneth Grahame.

  (Twayne's English authors series ; TEAS 449)
  Bibliography: p.
  Includes index.
    1. Grahame, Kenneth, 1859–1932—Criticism and
interpretation.   2. Children's stories, English—
History and criticism.   I. Title.   II. Series.
PR4727.K88   1987   828'.809   87-405
ISBN 0-8057-6943-9 (alk. paper)

Contents

About the Author

Lois Kuznets received her B.A. from Swarthmore College, her M.A.T. from Yale University, and her Ph.D. in medieval literature from Indiana University. She is an associate professor of English at San Diego State University, where she teaches both children's literature and medieval literature. She has published numerous articles on children's literature, including "Toad Hall Revisited," an application of Gaston Bachelard's phenomenological criticism to *The Wind in the Willows*. Her area of primary interest is the novel for the child of middle years. She is presently working on a study of modern British female fantasists for children.

Preface

Kenneth Grahame, known best for his children's classic, *The Wind in the Willows*, was neither a full-time nor a prolific writer. Urged by his most enthusiastic editor, W. E. Henley, to give up his position as gentleman-clerk at the Bank of England in order to devote himself to the craft, Grahame replied firmly that he was, as far as writing was concerned, "a spring not a pump."

So he remained a banker until he was forty-nine years old and rose to be secretary of the Bank of England, a prestigious post from which he retired shortly before the publication in 1908 of *The Wind in the Willows*. Originating supposedly in bedtime stories told to his son Alastair as early as 1904 and definitely in letters sent to Alastair during the summer of 1907, this animal fantasy is Grahame's only novel; it is also his last work of any substance. On this work (and to some extent a picture book, *The Reluctant Dragon*, extracted from a story for adults) rests his present reputation as a writer for children.

Preceding *The Wind in the Willows* were four slim volumes of prose for adults; most of their contents had first appeared piecemeal in periodicals between 1888 and 1898, along with incidental poems that no one but Grahame's official biographer, Patrick Chalmers, has made much effort to preserve. Yet the following study considers all of these prose works, as well as *The Wind in the Willows*, for they formed Grahame's reputation in his own time, a reputation not limited to his image as a fantasist for children. These earlier works give important insight into the development of his ideas and style, as well as into the nature of his influence on twentieth-century writers.

Only with the publication in the fall of 1893 of the first of these volumes, *Pagan Papers* (a collection of short personal essays followed by five short stories), did Grahame's name come to the attention of the reading audience. With a few exceptions, these pieces had previously appeared anonymously in Henley's *National Observer*. The essays did not seem particularly original to Grahame's contemporaries; they considered them largely as "Stevensonettes," that is, in the fashion of the essays of Robert Louis Stevenson. Like Stevenson's, in subject matter, if not in style, Grahame's pieces were concerned with various means of escape from the pressures of life in modern England. The following study makes no claim that *Pagan Papers* should be reissued, but does suggest that these early essays can provide insight into the origins of Grahame's nostalgia for a past Golden Age, revealing its connection with both nineteenth-century romanticism and the dualism implicit in late nineteenth-century neo-paganism. Not just ideas, but stylistic strategies are, however, also of concern. For this reason, separate essays receive detailed consideration in hope that the special flavor of Grahame's early prose will emerge, indicating in both its whimsical elusiveness and its density the promise it held for Grahame's fiction.

While reactions to *Pagan Papers* were mixed in Grahame's day, his next two books, *The Golden Age* (1895) and *Dream Days* (1898), met with almost instantaneous favor that spread far beyond the boundaries of England. Both were collections of semiautobiographical stories about five orphans living in a state of emotional neglect with various aunts and uncles. Following a hint given by Stevenson in an essay called "Child's Play," Grahame dubbed their guardians "Olympians" in the prologue to the series, which had appeared with the first five stories about these children in the first edition of *Pagan Papers*. The adversarial relationship between the dull, officious Olympians and the enlightened or "illuminati" children had unprecedented appeal for grown-up readers. Close examination of these two volumes reveals that the portrayal of childhood was not the only seductive element in these works; Grahame formed here his prevailing image of what an attractive grown-up life was: one that retained childlike wonder yet was endowed with all the power and privilege of a gentleman of leisure. He explores this gentlemanly life-style more fully in *The Wind in the Willows*, where it becomes central.

The Golden Age and *Dream Days* deserve examination in their own right. The following study explores a number of motifs in *The Golden Age* and finds that its sequel, *Dream Days*, while similar, also differs from the earlier volume in subtle but significant ways. The place of these stories in the development of the domestic or family novel in children's literature receives more attention here than in previous studies, with special emphasis on the elaboration of solitary daydreams and imaginative play. *The Golden Age* and *Dream Days* still make pleasurable reading, but the recent reissuing of these two books of stories attests perhaps more to a market of children's literature scholars than to a wider audience.

Published in book form in the same year as *Dream Days, The Heads-woman* first appeared in the *Yellow Book* in 1894. This fable for adults is a milestone in the development of Grahame's fiction, but one that points in a direction not taken by Grahame: fiction for adults with human adult protagonists. Considered by Grahame's contemporaries to be a humorous put-down of the women's rights movement, *The Headswoman* provides one key to Grahame's ambivalent attitude toward women, expressed in *The Wind in the Willows* by almost total exclusion of "the second sex."

Although Grahame's attitude toward women is not the central concern of the following study, the ways in which he connects nature with a paternal rather than maternal ideal is a matter of note in *The Wind in the Willows* and in several of Grahame's earlier works. This motif is, however, only one of many studied in *The Wind in the Willows,* which is here treated as a multilayered work of both substantive and formal complexity, despite the fact that it ostensibly addresses itself to children and despite Grahame's own claims to a kind of negative simplicity. The critics of Grahame in his own day did not do well with this book, perhaps because they took Grahame too much at his word that this was an animal tale with no political, social, or psychological implications. Both *The Wind in the Willows's* slow start—compared with the instantaneous popularity of *The Golden Age* and *Dream Days*—and its lasting fame rest on the complexity of Grahame's vision of the conflicts of modern life and the charm of his ameliorative resolution of these conflicts. *The Wind in the Willows* is fully a novel, not just a tale, and was certainly a hard act to follow for Grahame—who never really attempted to do so—and for subsequent creators of animal fantasy.

While working on this study, I met many Grahame enthusiasts, most of them American adults who associated their childhood reading of Grahame with both a family reading tradition and a British prose tradition that has guided their adult tastes in literature. They, in turn, have attempted to pass *The Wind in the Willows* on to their own children, perhaps not as successfully as did their parents, for the world changes rapidly as we approach the twenty-first century while the density of Grahame's style seems increasingly foreign to American children. Now, however, the book is also a staple of university classes in children's literature. When introduced in all its literary complexity, *The Wind in the Willows* sometimes captures the attention and devotion of students who have never before encountered it and who find it a testament to their own ambivalent participation in a technologically complex world, a book that thus "speaks to their condition" and anticipates their longings for a simpler life seemingly closer to Father Nature.

Lois R. Kuznets

San Diego State University

Acknowledgments

First published in 1959 and commemorating the centennial of Kenneth Grahame's birth, Peter Green's biography delineates the conflictual forces that formed and acted upon Grahame as a complex man of his time and station, as well as the ways in which these pressures are reflected in all of his works. Everyone who writes about Grahame after the appearance of Green's volume of scholarly research and masterly analysis must acknowledge Green's contribution in this area, just as one must be thankful for Patrick Chalmers's official biography of Grahame, appearing in 1933, one year after Grahame's death; the latter gathered together many hitherto unpublished or uncollected pieces. I have certainly benefited from these two biographies, but I wish to make special acknowledgment of the influence that Peter Green's work has had on my study, not only in terms of factual information, but in terms of critical interpretation.

Unlike Green, however, I come to Grahame's work with a background in children's literature and have attempted to give special attention to Grahame's place as a writer for and about children. My reflections in this area have been both materially and spiritually aided by the support of many colleagues in the Children's Literature Association, too numerous to name, and especially my close friends, Anita Moss and Phyllis Bixler. I am grateful to Ruth MacDonald for first telling me about this project and to Priscilla Ord for sending me an encouraging talisman. Jim Blodgett, with whom I also share the field of medieval literature, lent his discerning ear to some of my early chapters. Alethea Helbig, Fred Peters, and Marcia Shafer were of great help in obtaining books until I was granted generous library privileges as a visiting scholar at the University of Michigan. Jerry Griswold and Jim Gellert kindly helped polish the manuscript.

Two others with whom I can no longer share this book helped to make it possible: my dear mother-in-law, Marion B. Dowling (1905–84), who read the first pages of this manuscript with her usual critical acumen, and my beloved aunt, Celia D. Rostow (1899–1985), who, long ago, took on a semiorphaned child and gave her the lifetime of emotional support that Grahame missed from his Olympians.

KENNETH GRAHAME

This book was written with the help of a two-year grant-in-aid from my husband, Jim Dowling, and that was the least of his giving. It is dedicated to him and my daughters, Naomi and Miriam Kuznets, with love.

Chronology

convalescing from severe illness. Marries Elspeth Thomson in Fowey, 22 July.

1900   Son, Alastair Grahame, born 12 May.

1904   Begins to tell Alastair bedtime stories about some of *The Wind in the Willows* creatures.

1906   Moves back to Cookham Dene.

1907   "Bertie's Escapade," for Alastair's newspaper. Writes series of letters to Alastair, May–September. Visited by Constance Smedley of *Everybody's,* who urges him to develop animal stories.

1908   Resigns from the Bank of England. *The Wind in the Willows.*

1910   Buys old farmhouse, Boham's, Blewbury, Berkshire.

1913   "The Fellow That Goes Alone," essay.

1916   Edits and introduces *The Cambridge Book of Poetry for Children.*

1920   Alastair Grahame run over by a train, possible suicide. The Grahames leave for the Continent, October, where they travel for some four years, centering on Rome.

1921   "Ideals," lecture to Keats-Shelley Society in Rome.

1924   Returns to England to Church Cottage, Pangbourne, where he remains for rest of life.

1925   Introduction to George Sanger's *Seventy Years a Showman.*

1930   Attends performance of A. A. Milne's *Toad of Toad Hall.*

1931   E. H. Shepard visits Grahame at Pangbourne to make sketches for new edition of *The Wind in the Willows.* "A Dark Star," lecture. "Oxford Through a Boy's Eyes," essay, published posthumously.

1932   Grahame dies at Pangbourne, 6 July.

Chapter One
Living a Life East of Eden

Children—if they think about the subject at all—may imagine writers of their favorite books leading lives similar to those led by the characters in their beloved stories. Only the most naive adult, however, might picture Kenneth Grahame as actually living the life he claimed to depict in *The Wind in the Willows,* a life of "sunshine, running water, woodlands, dusty roads, winter firesides, free of problems, clear of the clash of sex. . . ."[1] Nor did Grahame ever lead a simple, carefree existence even when he finally had the financial resources to approximate that life.

Instead, Grahame experienced a childhood full of personal loss and emotional neglect; an early scholastic success followed not by the academic or rural life that he desired, but by the necessity of earning his living in the heart of London; a writing career carried on almost simultaneously with his business career and in sophisticated literary circles; a late marriage disappointing in itself and finally tragic in its issue; a grand literary success that left him free to act out, unsuccessfully, that imaginary life, "free of problems," and a quiet death after some twenty-five years of little literary import.

In short, Kenneth Grahame, like both his adult and child readers, led a complex life, east of Eden. Not the least of interest here is the way in which his works, in spite of Grahame's own protestations of simplicity, reflect this complexity.

Childhood and Schooling 1859–76

The physical landscape of Grahame's early childhood was more rugged than the downs and riverbanks of south-central England depicted in his books. His psychic landscape was even more rugged—full of upheaval and continuing traumatic loss of precious people and places.

Grahame was a Scot, born on 8 March 1859 in Edinburgh, a city of dark stone buildings overlooked by a romantic castle on a hill. At the foot of this hill and facing the site of Sir Walter Scott's former home was the upper-middle-class house of Bessie Ingles Grahame and James Cunningham Grahame, Kenneth's parents. This house in its respectable Castle Street neighborhood stood for the solidity of the Grahames' Scots Calvinist background, centered professionally in finance and the law. So that when, a year after Kenneth's birth, his father took his sociable young wife and their three children to Argyllshire in western Scotland, where he assumed the post of sheriff-substitute, James Grahame was in all probability already acknowledging some failure or discouragement. He was an advocate with fine family connections and a reputation as a bon vivant, but his Edinburgh career was perhaps not as brilliant as expected.

At a year old, Kenneth was little affected by this first move, however hard it was for his parents. The young Grahames, Helen, then four, and Thomas William (Willie), then two, as well as Kenneth, enjoyed the environs of Loch Fyne in the two port towns where the Grahames rented houses for three years while a home was being built for the family in Inveraray. Kenneth's main memories of these early years centered on the waterfront. His love for water and for "messing about in boats" was deep-seated, first formed in relation to the salt water of these Loch ports. The rugged countryside of Argyllshire, home of the Campbell clan, did not make as much of an impression on him as landscapes in which he was later allowed to roam more freely.

In the spring of 1864, less than a year after the Grahames had moved into their substantial new home in Inveraray, the children suffered their most severe trauma. Kenneth was barely five when, two weeks after the birth of her fourth child, Roland, Bessie Grahame came down with scarlet fever and died. Kenneth too caught scarlet fever. His maternal grandmother, Granny Ingles, arrived to nurse him and to help her stricken son-in-law, who never recovered from the loss of his wife and did virtually nothing to help his children recover from it.

What James Grahame did do was to shift all of the burden of caretaking and much of the financial responsibility as well onto the shoulders of Granny Ingles, who was later aided financially by Kenneth's uncle, John Grahame. Kenneth's father seems to have sunk into both depression and alcoholism.

Shortly after Kenneth's recovery, Granny Ingles, then in her sixties, moved with the three young children and the newborn infant into a large house, the Mount, Cookham Dene, far south of Argyllshire, in Berkshire, on the Thames River. Kenneth did not form a strong attachment to his grandmother, who is reputed to have treated the children correctly but coldly; he certainly, however, bound himself emotionally to the Mount and its surroundings. This place figured strongly in his memories of the period between the years of four and seven, years that he later described as most influential in his consciousness of self throughout his life.[2]

What Grahame's biographers say about this period is mainly garnered from autobiographical interpretations of Grahame's *The Golden Age* and *Dream Days,* with some emendations from his sister, Helen. The many differences between the fictional family depicted there and Grahame's own make such interpretations risky. Clearly, although Kenneth had a relationship with his maternal uncle, the Reverend David Ingles, he found no parent substitutes in his semiorphaned state and developed a distrust of relatives that outlasted his general distrust of "Olympians" (as he dubs adults in these two books). Kenneth's fondness of solo rambles through the countryside also grew during those mid-childhood days, while certain aspects of the roomy house pervaded his imagination.

The peace and pleasant stimulation that Kenneth found at the Mount permeated later memories, but were short-lived. Within two years, financial difficulties dictated a move from the large interesting house into a smaller cottage in Cranbourne. Then James Grahame's paternal instincts came briefly back to life and he brought the four children to Inveraray for almost a year beginning in the spring of 1866. At the end of that year, when Kenneth's father left for the Continent never to return, the children were shipped back to Granny Ingles in Cranbourne. Of his children only Kenneth, the oldest living son, attended James Grahame's funeral in Le Havre some twenty-one years later. No evidence exists of contact between father and children in the intervening years. Grahame never mentions either parent in his published works.

The next upheaval in Kenneth's life was the traditional one of English schoolboys of the upper classes—going away to school. He shared this transition with his older brother, Willie. After several years of private and probably sporadic tutoring, in 1868 both were enrolled at the relatively late ages of nine and ten in St. Edward's School in Oxford. Years later in an essay published posthumously, "Oxford Through a Boy's Eyes," Grahame describes the confusion, excitement, and trepidation of his arrival and also his later delight in exploring.[3] The rigidity we are led to expect from many school novels of the nineteenth century was not generally true of his experience there. St. Edward's was then a relatively new school, more flexible in its supervision of the boys than the older traditional public schools of England. After some hard adjustments, Kenneth spent the next seven years proving himself to be an excellent scholar and athlete. The architecture and environs of Oxford, like those of the Mount, Cookham Dene, obviously suited him. Kenneth had time to roam the gardens of Oxford and to continue his loving relationship with the river Thames, which runs through Oxford as it does through Cookham Dene, and indeed through most of Grahame's life.

Unlike many budding authors, Grahame seems to have been neither a child storyteller nor a scribbler. No child in the imaginary family he created for *The Golden Age* is really a writer either. Kenneth was, however, during his youth, known to recite bits of long narrative poems aloud as he rambled through the countryside. Only one piece of writing emerges from these years, a conventional schoolboy essay.[4]

Willie Grahame died of a respiratory ailment at the age of sixteen. Little is known about Grahame's relationship with this brother, only one year older than he, and his companion at St. Edward's. Grahame may even have become defensively immune to the loss of intimates before Willie died. Willie's death signaled a gathering cloud of stressful change although Kenneth's final year at St. Edwards was triumphant; he was then "head (or captain) of school" (an appointed post of both honor and power) and had won prizes for accomplishments in areas ranging from rugby to divinity.

Not unnaturally, Kenneth had, on the basis of his own achievements rather than the family pattern, great expectations of continuing at Oxford after St. Edward's. Neither his grandmother nor his Uncle John was prepared to reward his accomplishments in this way. Instead, Kenneth left school at sixteen and was put on the waiting list for the post of gentleman-clerk at the Bank of England. This meant London rather than Oxford, another abrupt and uncongenial change in dwelling as far as Kenneth was concerned, since he certainly preferred the groves of academe to the looming temples of the money-changers.

On one level, Grahame's childhood and schooldays were times on which he could look back as a "golden age." This nostalgia was largely centered on places rather than people; it rested also on his own competence in finding congenial ways of occupying himself. But deep familial relationships as he knew them could not be trusted to remain constant, stable, and emotionally fulfilling. His personal experience of emotional deprivation and disappointment at not being permitted to follow the line of his ambition and interest also contributed to his distrust of the examples of mid-Victorian society whom he knew well. As it happens, although Grahame's specific personal circumstances were painful, this particular distrust of this particular generation was quite widespread among Grahame's contemporaries. In writing, it often took the form of a type of social satire. This satirical note also reflects the enormous changes in English thought, institutions, and society beginning to emerge in the latter half of the nineteenth century, which came to a head by the end of World War I. Grahame would turn out later to be conservative about many of these changes, yet some place in his thinking, if not his actions, the losses and disappointments of his childhood translated themselves into rebellion. He went to London as a mid-Victorian who knew where his duty lay, but also as a disgruntled adolescent.[5]

The London Apprenticeship 1876–93

London has always been a fascinating city and young adults usually have strong recuperative powers. So Grahame made an acceptable life for himself in London, or rather, it seems, made two potential lives. On the one hand, he did what was expected of him by his family and worked successfully to advance his career as a bourgeois city man; on the other hand, he led a life of the mind that brought him into literary circles and stimulated his own writing, opening opportunities to become a "bohemian" author.

While waiting for a gentleman-clerk's opening at the Bank of England, Kenneth was expected to work for his Uncle John's firm of parliamentary agents in Westminster. It is unclear what his duties were, but he did spend some of this time learning shorthand. Shorthand was a skill used mainly by political reporters of the time; Grahame, stimulated by parliamentary activities, may have thought briefly of this type of journalism.[6] He did not follow it through after 1 January 1879 when he joined the bank, having received "full points"—an unusually high grade—on an entrance essay.

He lodged during the initial period of waiting with his Uncle Robert Grahame, in Fulham, a relatively green and suburban part of London at the time. One relative whom he saw there, his cousin, Annie Grahame, became a firm friend; she had perhaps also romantic leanings toward Kenneth that were never fulfilled (although it is possible that they were reciprocated).[7] When he joined the bank, Grahame took a closer flat on Bloomsbury Street, which he eventually shared with his younger brother, Roland, when he too came to work there. By 1882, however, Grahame was able to take single lodgings and found a flat on the top floor of 65 Chelsea Gardens. It was cramped but afforded him a view of his beloved Thames and of Battersea Park. To some of his guests it resembled the aerie of a lighthouse.

A portion of his spare hours was spent in two nonliterary pursuits appropriate to his young city-man image. He drilled with the London Scottish Regiment and did charitable work with a workingman's association, Toynbee Hall. The former gave him a chance to show off an impressive physique in kilts and to participate in such public events as Queen Victoria's Jubilee Day. At Toynbee Hall, where he directed several athletic activities, he could keep in shape.

There was much extra time. Bankers' hours were indeed short and the life of a gentleman clerk not strenuous; surprisingly, the Old Lady of Threadneedle Street, as the bank was familiarly called, was not staid. Long lunches with heavy drinking and other indulgences were the rule rather than the exception.[8] Grahame had plenty of time for one of his own indulgences, sight-seeing, to which he was never averse in urban areas where he could not roam the countryside.

Evenings were spent exploring too. Grahame developed a lifelong passion for Italian cooking, available at many little restaurants in Soho. At one of these, he casually encountered the eminent scholar F. J. Furnivall, founder of the Early English Text Society, with his usual group of disciples. Grahame swiftly became a protégé of his, not only in the many literary activities that Furnivall organized and directed, but also in sculling, a boating enthusiasm shared by Grahame.

Through his contact with Furnivall, Grahame, still in his late teens, found some of the intellectual stimulation and direction that he would have found at Oxford. His reading was expanded into English medieval works; he met key literary figures of the day, such as Tennyson and Browning, as well as newer writers. He became, in 1880, at the age of twenty-one, honorary secretary of the Shakespeare Society founded by Furnivall and, in 1887, acted in a production of Shelley's *The Cenci,* put on by the then-daring Shelley Society, also founded by Furnivall.

Some time after he started to work for the Bank of England, Grahame began to use a bank ledger in which to record both poetry and prose. These fragments confirm the judgment of Furnivall, who, when Grahame showed him this book, advised Grahame to stick to prose.[9] Apparently, Furnivall's blunt judgment was not discouraging to Grahame, who later published a few poems, but concentrated on prose.

New places began to feed Grahame's imagination as he took lengthy vacations during the 1880s. In 1884, with his sister Helen, he enjoyed the coast of Cornwall. In 1886, he visited his Uncle Robert's villa in Tuscany. The South, as epitomized by Italy, attracted him for its real and symbolic contrasts to the land where he had grown up; during his bachelor days, he took frequent trips to the Continent.

One grim duty that he had to perform during this period was to attend his father's funeral in Le Havre and deal with such meager portable property as his father then possessed. Grahame brought back little of his father's. Yet James Grahame's death seems to have heralded a sudden freedom on Kenneth's part to submit his writing for publication.[10]

At first, he submitted these pieces anonymously, with the exception of a few poems. Because of this anonymity, earlier works are hard to trace. On Boxing Day, 26 December 1888, in the *St. James's Gazette,* the first definitely attributable prose item appeared, a word sketch of the Berkshire Downs in winter, "By a Northern Furrow." Grahame started slowly. His next essay was published in the same evening paper in September of 1890.[11]

Within that year, Grahame had also submitted some items to the *Scots Observer,* the first of which was published in October. With this submission began another influential literary relationship; this one was with William Ernest Henley, the *Observer's* editor, soon to move to London himself and call his journal the *National Observer.* Like Furnivall, Henley was quick to notice and enlist young talent. He soon gathered around him in London a group known as "Henley's Young Men." For Henley, author of the popular poem "Invictus" (1875), was a brilliant and witty talker, rivaled only perhaps by his "enemies," Oscar Wilde and George Bernard Shaw. The former he fought for his "decadence," the latter for his socialism.

Henley's philosophy combined political conservatism with activist individualism; it fitted Grahame's own ideas well. The rebellion

against organized Christianity and the agnosticism that were a part of
Henley's world view were also in line with the nature of the Grahame's rebellion. Not only did Grahame continue to write for and
publish in the *National Observer,* but he added a distinguished and
handsome, if reserved, presence to the group that gathered around
Henley socially. Grahame also managed to stay on Henley's good side
although the latter was known for fits of anger and feuds.[12]

Henley was not only a brilliant talker but a brilliant editor. He
attracted many remarkable writers to the *National Observer,* among
them Yeats, Conrad, Crane, James, and H. G. Wells, (and even G.
B. Shaw). Grahame was in good company. In the next two years,
Henley published some twenty-one pieces by Grahame in the *National
Observer,* all anonymously. Then Henley suggested that Grahame
gather together these essays and submit them to John Lane of the
Bodley Head Press. They were published as *Pagan Papers* in a small
first edition in October of 1893. This edition had a frontisplace by
Aubrey Beardsley depicting the god Pan, in loose shirt and tie, gazing speculatively and suggestively at a faun—a depiction of Pan in no
way like that of the text. This edition also included six pieces separately entitled "The Golden Age." These were omitted in later editions and became part of Grahame's subsequent work.

Pagan Papers, in its final form, consisted of eighteen personal essays, generally short and light in tone. Their subject matter was not
unusual—reflections upon such pastimes as smoking and country
walks. A few, to later readers at least, were not as light as they at
first seemed and expressed real bitterness and anger at life in the modern world. The "paganism" and "bohemianism" embodied in them
were peculiar to late nineteenth-century England. Reviews of *Pagan
Papers* were mixed. Many noted Grahame's belonging to Henley's
group and also compared his work to Robert Louis Stevenson's essays,
not always favorably. With this work, no matter what its reception,
Grahame emerged from obscurity to become a talent worth watching
and cultivating.

In 1893, Grahame was thirty-four years old. He was steadily rising
in the Bank of England and had published his first book. Clearly tal-
ented, he had found inspiring literary mentors in Furnivall and Henley. Henley encouraged Grahame at this point to give up the bank
and engage in writing full time. Grahame refused, with the later often quoted description of himself as "a spring not a pump."[13] Behind
this image lurks the idea of the "gentleman author," who writes only

because he is inspired rather than driven by necessity. Grahame could cling to this ideal of authorship because—in following his family's wishes rather than his own academic desires—he had found one way of supporting himself securely in a relatively leisurely job with status. Not a man of independent means, Grahame yet had time for intellectual and social pursuits, travel, and, when inspired, writing. The two lives he led thus seemed to enrich each other and approximate that of the "gentleman author." To give up one of them must then have appeared dangerous and unnecessary. Apparently Grahame was not ready as yet to risk change in his dual professional life or, for that matter, his personal life as an eligible, sought after, and somewhat elusive bachelor. [14]

The Peak Years 1894–1908

In the 1890s, Grahame's star was ascendant. Before the decade was over, he had crowned his literary success with the publication of two more books; in 1898, at thirty-nine, he became a relatively young secretary of the Bank of England; in 1899, at forty, he became a not-so-young bridegroom.

After the publication of *Pagan Papers*, Grahame continued to widen his literary circle. The *National Observer* under Henley failed, perhaps because it was too advanced in a literary sense for the conservative readers that Henley's politics attracted. [15] In the literary world the *Observer* also had a new competitor, the *Yellow Book*, which published—in spite of its ostensible philosophical differences from the *National Observer*—works of many of the same fine new talents, including pieces by Kenneth Grahame.

Misunderstandings about both Grahame's philosophy and the stance of the *Yellow Book* make it hard to imagine Grahame's associating himself in publication, let alone socially, with the *Yellow Book* group; yet he did both for about a year. The *Yellow Book*, so-called because its yellow cover was intended to evoke associations with risqúe French novels, had a popular reputation for scandalizing and fin de siècle decadence that reflects neither its content nor the real life-style of its literary editor and most of its contributors. Aubrey Beardsley's illustrations were often more suggestive than the texts themselves.

When begun in 1894, the *Yellow Book*—with American novelist Henry Harland as literary editor and Beardsley as art editor—while embracing aestheticism, tried hard to steer away from those of its chief exponents such as Oscar Wilde, who were considered "decadent." Beardsley himself was dropped later (and perhaps too late) in order to avoid any scandalous reputation. The magazine indulged in only mild spasms of *épater les bourgeois;* its antipuritanism was shared by W. E. Henley himself. Its art-for-art's-sake posture really repelled the activist Henley, but Grahame seemed relatively comfortable at first with the *Yellow Book's* point of view. After the trial and imprisonment of Oscar Wilde for homosexuality, however, Grahame moved away from this group as did many others, since it was obviously associated with a like "decadence" in the minds of the public at least.

One interesting piece of Grahame's that appeared in the *Yellow Book,* in 1894, was "The Headswoman," later published in book form. This satiric piece is the only one of Grahame's works of fiction that deals principally with human adults. Its view of women and women's rights is interesting and complex.

Grahame was a fairly skillful satirist, but certainly not a leader in this area of writing. His true bent as well as contribution came rather with his last three books. The first two of these, *The Golden Age* (1895) and *Dream Days* (1898), through a series of brief stories, create a fictitious family of five children, one of whom is the narrator looking back on his childhood with some distance—but not too much. Henley usually gets the credit for encouraging this strain in Grahame's writing.[16]

Selina, Edward, an unnamed male narrator, Harold, and Charlotte, won the hearts of many, including not only Swinburne but also Teddy Roosevelt and the German Kaiser. The sense of a gap between the sensitive imaginative child and the plodding adult Olympian is certainly a product here of nineteenth-century romantic views of childhood, clearly expressed, for instance, in such works as Wordsworth's "Ode: Intimations of Immorality." But Grahame avoids the sentimentality of some of Wordsworth's followers. The incidents he creates are both realistic in detail and often funny. Although not books written for children, they have to some extent been influenced by Grahame's reactions, both positive and negative, to books written previously for and about children. They, in turn, have had considerable influence on the family novel for children. After their publication, Grahame came to be considered an authority on children's literature. Editors sought him to review new books and to introduce and edit collections of such works as Eugene Fields's poems for children and Billinghurst's version of Aesop's fables.

Unlike his cousin, A. H. Hawkins, who during this period gave up his practice of law to devote himself full time to writing under the pen name of Anthony Hope (author of *The Prisoner of Zenda*), Grahame clung to the bank. All of the above works, except the last portion of *The Wind in the Willows*, were written while Grahame was still rising, finally to become the bank's secretary, a post part managerial and part public relations. The secretary was the main liaison between the board and the governor of the bank. By and large, Grahame kept his business and his literary worlds separate. It is said that for a long time the governor of the bank was under the misapprehension that Grahame's *The Golden Age* was a book about bullion. Others more knowledgeable felt somewhat displeased that their secretary was spending his free time in this way.[17]

During this period Grahame was feeling secure enough to add more style to his personal life. In 1894, he took a townhouse, 5 Kensington Crescent, with a barrister friend, Tom Greg, and a housekeeper, Sarah Bath. They led a gracious life. Grahame began to collect antiques. He continued his trips to Italy, going to the Riviera in 1895. With his sister, on other vacations, he also returned to Cornwall, where he made two firm friends in the port town of Fowey.

Each of these men represented in some way the variety Grahame sought in his extrabusiness life. One of them was Arthur Quiller-Couch, a family man who combined academic pursuits with the writing of popular adventure novels. The other was Edward Atkinson, a bachelor of about sixty when Grahame met him. Atkinson was a gentleman of independent means who owned a house in Fowey, thirty boats, and a collection of old toys. All of these—the house, the boats, the toys—Grahame found fascinating.

Possibly, Grahame was at his happiest and most fulfilled during this era. In his long bachelorhood he was never associated publicly with any woman, nor has it ever been implied that he was homosexual. Grahame seems to have held rather romantic views of women, and perhaps was easily disillusioned by the real thing. Moreover, as many people noticed, he was not eager for intimacy. The bachelor's life was well suited to such a temperament, which was from childhood basically wary of human commitment.

Grahame was a large, well-built and exceedingly handsome man whom others, in his maturity, found charming but aloof. Most also found him curiously childlike and compared him variously to a startled faun, a St. Bernard, and a schoolboy.[18] All of these descriptions suggest a certain naiveté. Still, he was not particularly prudish in his reading or his writing. He read, enjoyed, and alluded to Rabelais, as many of his contemporaries did not. Also, Peter Green has discovered an anonymous piece of Grahame's, published in 1890, that uses in a disguised, playful form the bedroom scandal of the Irish leader Parnell and Mrs. O'Shea.[19] Nevertheless, reading and writing are not acting, and Grahame was clearly correct, reserved, and discreet—if not indeed repressed—in his social behavior.

Although he obviously participated in a sophisticated society, he also enjoyed the company of "simple" men—fishermen and farmers— and was pleased when they accepted him as a co-worker or drinking companion. Grahame's sense of equality did not go much deeper than that; he was known to express many of the common prejudices of his time, place, and station toward people of other nations and races as well as toward members of the English urban working class (who had none of the pastoral associations of the rural peasantry).[20]

Although Grahame looked strong, he was subject to severe bouts of illness, usually respiratory, throughout his life. In 1899, he was bedridden for a number of months, during which time his romance with Elspeth Thomson developed. She brought him grapes and sympathy while he was nursed at home by his sister and housekeeper. He, in turn, wrote her letters in baby talk which are, with hindsight, distressing to read.[21] Grahame and Thomson were wed in Fowey that summer. To practically all but the man and woman themselves, their marriage seemed an ill-match from the start to finish, although it lasted through mutual disappointment and bereavement until Grahame's death some thirty years later.

One of those fiercely opposed to their marriage, perhaps more selfishly than prophetically, was Fletcher Moulton, Elspeth's stepfather, a Liberal politician for whom she had been hostess from the time of her mother's death some ten years before. As hostess she had had, like Grahame, chances to meet with a number of prominent men of the day. She also took advantage of the opportunity to court some literary lions in an approximation of a salon. She too had some personal literary ambitions and, in 1888, under the pseudonym of Clarence Onslow, had published a penny novel entitled *Amelia Jane's Ambition.* By the time she met Grahame, which was probably sometime in 1897, she wrote poetry but seemed to see herself more as patron of the literary world than as author.

Elspeth Thomson was, at the time of their meeting, in her late thirties; she apparently affected, however, in spite of her social experience and responsibility, some "little girl" airs that initially seemed attractive to Grahame but were not as deep or sincere as his own boyish qualities. Very shortly after their wedding, she wrote despondent poems and letters to a friend that suggest she had come to the marriage with expectations that were not fulfilled. Grahame did not show such open unhappiness, but certain general statements that begin to appear on his part—such as his description of *The Wind in the Willows* are being "free from the clash of sex"—suggest the nature of the Grahames' incompatibility. The early years of their marriage give evidence of several lengthy, publicly unacknowledged, separations.

Sarah Bath, Grahame's housekeeper, also disapproved of the marriage and did not come with the newlyweds to their new house at 16 Durham Villas, Campden Hill. There, during the early years, Mrs. Grahame attempted to reestablish herself as a hostess, but received little cooperation from Grahame, who proved to be an absentminded and reluctant host. He seemed to prefer male companions. One of these was a new neighbor, Grahame Robertson, bachelor playwright and artist. Robertson's play, *Pinkie and the Fairies,* enjoyed contemporary popularity but has not stood the test of time; however, his belief and interest in the fairy folk might well have provided a tie with Grahame, who also admired Robertson's houseful of dogs. Grahame by this time had himself acquired a collection of toys that dominated his study and, according to Robertson (who did not disapprove), made it look like a nursery.[22]

Within a year of the marriage, in May 1900, the Grahames' only child, Alastair, was born, blind in one eye and with a squint in the other. His doting mother and his to some extent doting father made much of Alastair, tending to ignore his disabilities even in later years when they interfered severely with many of his activities. In the early years of his life, they kept track of his childish sayings and encouraged him to be aggressively articulate in adult society. At first, Alastair—nicknamed Mouse—certainly helped to hold his parents together; as he grew up and developed a number of problems, their own conflict not only probably aggravated his difficulties but often took the form of competition for his attention and regard.

One sore point in their relationship may have been Grahame's low

level of literary creativity in the years immediately following the marriage. He was in contact with his publisher, John Lane of Bodley
Head, and read some manuscripts for him, but the flow of writing
had temporarily stopped. In his role of secretary, his duties at the
bank were not onerous, so that this aridity could not be attributed to
that cause alone. As a matter of fact, there were suggestions from
Grahame's bank colleagues that Grahame was also not a very good
secretary during this period—neglectful and unambitious.[23]

In 1903, however, one rather spectacular event cast Grahame in a
hero's role at the bank. A respectable-looking but psychotic visitor
fired a gun at him. The intruder was finally cornered and subdued in
the director's library. Although in retrospect, the affair had its comical aspects, its violence was also disturbing; the man's purported alli-
ance with socialist causes hardened Grahame's political conservatism.
The only other noted event at the bank before Grahame's resignation
in June 1908 was the surprise visit of King George's four children in
1907. This is one of the few times that Grahame is publicly associated with children other than his own son.

In 1906, prior to his leaving the bank, the small family moved to
Cookham Dene—the area that Grahame loved so much as a child.
They first took one rented house and then leased a substantial one,
called Mayfield. Grahame commuted for a time, until he retired at
the age of forty-nine, pleading ill health.

Although Grahame's marriage may well have been the cause of
writer's block, his son indeed proved to be the direct stimulus, if not
the inspiration for, *The Wind in the Willows.* In his earlier works, Grahame had occasionally taken the points of view of animals, birds, and
even inanimate objects; "The Reluctant Dragon," originally published as a story in *Dream Days,* showed his talent in the development
of appealing nonhuman characters. What other stories he may previously have produced for Alastair are not known, because unre-
corded, but Grahame mentioned in a letter the beginning of a new
bedtime story for Alastair on the occasion of his fourth birthday. This
story seems to have been the seed from which *The Wind in the Willows*
eventually grew; it featured a mole, a giraffe, and a rat.[24] Later the
giraffe was replaced by Toad, who had certainly become an established favorite by 1907; both father and son identified Toad in certain
ways with son himself. Toad was thus the principal character in letters that Grahame wrote to Alastair in May of that year, when the
parents and son went on separate vacations. These letters continued

after all had returned, for Grahame spent the rest of the summer in London, in the Durham Villa house that they still maintained there, while mother and son remained in Cookham Dene. Alastair's governess, Miss Stott, fortunately saved these letters. They contained episodes that eventually appeared as chapters 6, 8, and 10–12 in *The Wind in the Willows*. They inspired Constance Smedley, European representative of the American magazine *Everybody's*, to urge Grahame to pull together his masterpiece.

Under ordinary circumstances, Smedley would probably never have obtained an initial interview with Grahame; she, however, made a whimsical approach to him that worked beautifully: she wrote him a letter claiming to be a relative of Miss Smedley, the fictitious governess of the fictitious children in *The Golden Age* and *Dream Days*. Grahame not only agreed to see her, but also found her empathetic and confided in her about his work. Her insistence and the promise that *Everybody's* would publish it made him finally complete a manuscript in 1908. This manuscript incorporated the letters that Smedley had first seen into much new material; it originally went under the name of "Mr. Toad," then "The Wind in the Reeds" and various other titles. [25]

Ironically, nobody wanted the completed manuscript. Not only did *Everybody's* refuse it, but so did Grahame's original publisher, John Lane of Bodley Head. This animal fantasy was not like Grahame's earlier successes: it was apparently written for children, not for adults who wanted to reminisce about childhood. Teddy Roosevelt, to whom Grahame sent a copy, was disappointed at first, but was instrumental in getting Scribner's unenthusiastically to publish it in America after Methuen, in England, took it with no greater enthusiasm. Reviewers could not make out just what kind of book it was. Once everyone accepted the change in subject matter, the book took off. For, although Grahame himself refused to acknowledge any but the most superficial readings of *The Wind in the Willows*, the story of Toad's, Mole's, and Rat's adventures alone and in the company of other River Bank and Wild Woods creatures has a universal appeal that suggests various levels of meaning, not all of which are accessible to children, or to adults for that matter, on the first reading.

The Wind in the Willows has sold well over the years, yet in 1959 Green wrote, "hardly anything has been written about [Grahame]." [26] This is no longer the case, for a new surge of scholarly and critical interest in children's literature emerged in the 1970s; with it *The*

Wind in the Willows received renewed attention as a children's classic, in the ranks of *Alice's Adventures in Wonderland* and *The Adventures of Tom Sawyer*. Not only has its longevity far exceeded that of some of the works that clearly influenced it, notably Richard Jefferies's *Wood Magic,* but *The Wind in the Willows* has, in turn, certainly influenced A. A. Milne's Christopher Robin stories and Tolkien's *The Hobbit.* Its complexity probably accounts for both *The Wind in the Willows*'s relatively slow start and its lasting power through nearly a century of changes more rapid (and more abhorrent) than any Grahame could have imagined.

Fortunately for Grahame, he could, by 1908, live on his past earnings and royalties, thus becoming a "country gentleman." He did not, however, become a gentleman author. His son's childhood and the Grahames' return to Cookham Dene enabled him briefly and fruitfully to overcome the effects of whatever disillusionment he felt with marriage and the bank, and to produce his masterpiece, but did not sustain further literary creativity.

The After Years 1908–32

To an immediate observer, the idea that the rest of Grahame's life was a poor ending would no doubt have seemed absurdly pessimistic, for, at the beginning of this period, Grahame, who seemed to have achieved one of his heart's main desires—to be free of city life—was also much admired and lionized by the literary world. With hindsight, however, one might view these years as generally a period of increasing isolation not only from the literary world but from people in general and from Grahame's two siblings, with whom he quarreled. He seemed little inspired to write and produced only upon request for an occasion. The elder Grahames' incompatibility resulted in an odd and eccentric household increasingly unsociable and almost miserly. As Alastair grew, his problems grew. Personal tragedy struck twice with the loss in 1911 of Grahame's Fowey friend, Atkinson, in a boating accident and then, in 1920, of Alastair, run over by a train.

Because their Mayfield lease ran out, the Grahames did not remain long in Cookham Dene after the publication of *The Wind in the Willows,* but bought an ancient farmhouse, Boham's, in Blewbury, on the Berkshire Downs, away from the Thames and more isolated than before. Their eccentric life-style eventually discouraged weekend visitors, but Grahame kept up a correspondence with some old friends. They did participate relatively actively in the village life around them, where Elspeth's eccentricity in conversation, eating habits, and dress made her something of a local character; Grahame, however, once won a shoulder of mutton at the Blewbury Fair in the "handsomest man" competition.[27]

During this period and in the midst of developing worries over Alastair, Grahame engaged in his first writing to be published after *The Wind in the Willows,* a piece entitled "The Fellow That Goes Alone."[28] Returning to the essay form (that of all his subsequent writing), Grahame here expresses the pleasures of solitude in the country.

In 1911, Alastair, who was developing from a rather fey child into an articulate, but awkwardly heavy boy, went off to school at the Old Malthouse; this was a good experience for the two years he spent there since the school was easygoing without undue emphasis on either scholarship or athletics, pursuits in which Alastair was handicapped by eyesight problems. Unfortunately, the choices that the Grahames made for Alastair's secondary education were not as wise. Alastair's early adolescence was marked by both severe acne and social awkwardness with his peers; he was still unscholarly and unathletic. Yet the Grahames, ignoring the advice of friends, sent him first to Rugby and then to Eton. He lasted six months at the former and a year at the latter. He returned in 1915 from these two traditional public schools showing signs of severe emotional stress. He was tutored at home from then on and was finally able to enter Christ Church, Oxford, in 1918.

This university admission was not the end of Alastair's difficulties. His emotional problems continued and took the form of a religious crisis in the months prior to his death. On 7 May 1920, after completing university examinations with no great distinction and just a few days before his twentieth birthday, he went for a walk at dusk; his mangled body was later discovered on the railroad tracks. The subsequent inquest arrived at a verdict of accidental death and attributed his being in the path of a train to his semiblindness. Certainly none of the Grahames' contemporaries wanted to pursue the question of suicide. The injuries that Alastair's body sustained, however, were in line with his having lain down on the tracks, not with his having been hit standing up.[29]

The Grahames could not sublimate this loss in other activities as they had apparently been able to do with previous disappointments and losses. Earlier, for instance, Grahame seems to have found some relief from his mourning of his friend, Atkinson, by working for the World War I effort, drilling a local troup, an occupation to which he applied himself with considerable enthusiasm. Then Alastair and Grahame seem to have had a brief period of real closeness when Grahame took his fourteen-year-old son on a trip to Scotland for the first time. Also, in 1916, Grahame enjoyed the publication of *The Cambridge Book of Children's Poetry,* which he had edited and introduced. But now, in the face of the ambiguous death of their troubled son, nothing in England could provide the Grahames with distraction, let alone comfort. Devastated by this loss, in 1921 the Grahames rented Boham's out and went to the Continent together for the first time since 1910. (After his marriage, Grahame had almost ceased going abroad and, when he did so, usually contrived to go alone.) They stayed there, mainly in Rome, for almost four years.

Although the years abroad did not stimulate much writing, they revived some of Grahame's earlier interests. Visitors to Rome described Grahame as an indefatigable guide to the sights of the city. As in his early London days, he sought out little restaurants and enjoyed good Mediterranean food, as well as wine. He delivered some lectures; one, on "Ideals," for the Keats-Shelley society of Rome, was published in 1922.[30] Other than the preface to *The Cambridge Book of Poetry,* this was Grahame's first published work since "The Felowe That Goes Alone" appeared in the *St. Edward's School Chronicle* in 1913.

On their return to England in 1924, the Grahames sold Boham's and moved to Church Cottage, Pangbourne, back again on the Thames. Here, in 1931, E. H. Shepard, about to illustrate a new edition of *The Wind in the Willows,* came to visit Grahame. Grahame was already suffering from the circulatory problems that caused his death, and he had to send Shepard to explore the river bank on his own.[31] Shepard's illustrations thus reflect the Pangbourne portion of the Thames, rather than the Thames around Cookham Dene or the banks of Fowey River, which actually provided most of Grahame's inspiration. Nevertheless, Shepard's illustrations remain most closely associated with *The Wind in the Willows,* although a number of illustrators, including Parrish and Rackham, have been inspired by the story.

It seems no coincidence that Shepard was also the illustrator of A. A. Milne's Christopher Robin stories. Grahame certainly provided some of Milne's inspiration. Milne, in a sense, acknowledged his debt to Grahame by making a play out of *The Wind in the Willows,* entitled *Toad of Toad Hall* and produced in 1930. Many of Grahame's fans found that Milne's play did not do justice to the book as a whole, but Grahame, who attended one of the performances, was apparently satisfied.[32]

In 1925, Grahame wrote a reminiscing introduction to the autobiography of a traveling circus proprietor, George Sanger's *Seventy Years a Showman.*[33] This piece, the last work published during his lifetime, shows again some of Grahame's ability to recapture both the scenes and feelings of his youth. Two others, a solemn lecture about the nature of the relationship between an author and his contemporary audience, "The Dark Star," and a livelier piece, "Oxford Through a Boy's Eyes," were published posthumously.[34]

On 6 July, 1932, Grahame suffered a cerebral hemorrhage and died in bed. For several years he had been ailing with circulatory problems, to which his weight and propensity to overeat and overdrink contributed. On the night of his death, Grahame had retired with a copy of Sir Walter Scott's *The Talisman.* This seems especially appropriate deathbed reading for a man who had been born some seventy-three years before on Castle Hill Street, Edinburgh, across the street from the site of Sir Walter Scott's former home.

Looking back on the literary aridity of the last twenty-five years of Grahame's life, one should note that Grahame's commitment to writing had always been sporadic and never completely wholehearted. He found writing difficult, as he in later years told those who urged him to write more.[35] His deepest pleasures seemed to lie not in writing but in reading and in a number of nonintellectual pursuits: isolated roaming of the countryside, boating, collecting sundry objects, mingling and working with rural people, and, as the years went by, perhaps excessive eating and drinking. In addition, by the time of his retirement, Grahame was set in his ways and received little stimulus from new ideas or people. From his introduction to Sanger's book, one can see he did enjoy one modern development—the cinema—but again for its escape value and aid to fantasizing.[36] As will become apparent in the discussion of *Pagan Papers,* a definite escapist note appears regularly in Grahame's writing. Once financially secure, Grahame could actually escape into the pleasurable activities he had always liked best and may not, therefore, have needed some of the sublimatory resolution to conflict that writing seems to have given him.

When considering Grahame's state of mind during this period, one should probably adopt an attitude somewhere between the sweetness and light of his early biographer, Patrick Chalmers, and the gloom conveyed by his later biographer, Peter Green. Among serious problems and tragic deaths were also the many pleasurable activities in which Grahame had always taken solace. Moreover, by the time Grahame was fifty, he had produced four books, three of which were extremely well received. If Grahame himself was content with this literary achievement, perhaps we should consider his last years in light of his own words about Fothergill, the title character of Grahame's early essay, "A Bohemian in Exile": "After all, his gains may have outbalanced his losses . . . he doubtless chose wisely to enjoy life in his own way, and to gather from the fleeting days what bliss they had to give, nor spend them in toiling for a harvest to be reaped when he was dust" (P, 82). For Grahame, like Fothergill, was epicurean in his personal habits and stoic in his philosophy.

Chapter Two

Developing Thought and Style: *Pagan Papers* and Other Essays

Lovers of *The Wind in the Willows* will not necessarily be enthralled by *Pagan Papers,* the base of Grahame's early reputation. Since 1888, Grahame had been submitting poems and short essays—most published anonymously—to newspapers and periodicals. In 1893, at the urging of W. E. Henley, editor of the *National Observer* where most of the prose pieces had already appeared, Grahame publicly acknowledged his authorship by gathering and publishing these works under his own name. The first small edition of *Pagan Papers* began with an inappropriately suggestive frontispiece by Aubrey Beardsley, included eighteen essays on diverse topics, and ended with six pieces not included in subsequent editions; these were a prologue and five stories that appeared thereafter in *The Golden Age.*

Pagan Papers may seem thin and derivative, but the essays in this volume are worth examining here along with Grahame's other essays of the 1890s. They display clearly the philosophic background and influences that permeate his later works and some of the formal devices further developed in his fiction. The handful of occasional essays published after *The Wind in the Willows* are interesting principally because they substantiate certain biographical speculations and form an enlightening contrast to Grahame's earlier essays, while retaining some of the elements helpful in interpreting his fiction.

Major Influences

Grahame's essays are peppered with short quotations and allusions. Shakespeare, Dickens, Jonson, Marvell, Rabelais, Tennyson, Emerson, Whitman, and others are jumbled together in a casual, eclectic way appropriate to informal, conversational writing. These essays thus give evidence of wide reading and good memory, but one must

examine them closely in order to see which authors and ways of thinking had real meaning for Grahame.

The classical. One of the clearest classical influences, chiefly
apparent in *The Wind in the Willows,* is Homer's *Odyssey.* But there
are other reminders of Grahame's classical education at St. Edward's,
where he won prizes in Latin. These influences, both implicit and explicit in his early essays, are less immediately discernible.

In terms of his frequent preoccupation with nature and man's relationship to it as both steward and observer, Grahame, like many who
practiced the personal essay form, owes something to Vergil's *Georgics:* poetry about farming activities from a practical point of view.
Unlike the other, more artificial, branch of pastoral poetry that Vergil
(70–19 B.C.) practiced in his *Eclogues*—where the gentry in the guise
of shepherds and shepherdessess disport themselves and declaim upon
love—the *Georgics* depend upon a realism of landscape and love of the
soil, animal husbandry, and seasonal earthy events. The Vergilian influence may have been partly derivative, coming to Grahame through
other essayists, but Grahame's observation of nature and fondness for
botanical detail, while certainly not free of romanticizing and anthropomorphism, still owe something to this classical line.

He expressed sentiments similar to Vergil's "happy is he who
knows the rural Gods—Pan and old Sylvanus, and the sisterhood of
the nymphs."[1] And Grahame's most enduring philosophic strain was
in line with Vergil's words: "May the countryside and the gliding
streams content me. Lost to fame, let me love river and woodland."[2]
In his country retirement, his advocacy of moderation in all things,
accompanied by fierce patriotism, the gentle satirist Horace (65–8
B.C.) too provides a general philosophic model for Grahame.

Explicit and deep is Grahame's interest in the stoicism of Marcus
Aurelius, second-century Roman philosopher-king. Passages from
Aurelius's *Meditations* appear in English in Grahame's works. They are
used as jumping off points for discussion, clearly indicating a strong
familiarity with Aurelius's ideas, although these are sometimes
treated with levity in Grahame's early writing. The attraction of
Aurelius's stoicism in the face of worldly disappointment and of his
advocacy of a detached view becomes stronger for Grahame in his later
life.

In an essay probably written about 1890, set up in proof for the
National Observer, but eventually published only in Chalmers' biography, Grahame utters a sentiment worthy of Aurelius: "Achievement

ever includes defeat." But this aphorism appears in the midst of a whimsically graphic depiction of the funeral of his past hopes.[3] In "Romance of the Road," he quotes Aurelius's axiom, "A man ought to be seen by the gods . . . neither dissatisfied with anything nor complaining" (*P, 6–7*). Grahame seemed to be epicurean with regard to his habits, and frequently suggests in these essays that one may deal with worldly disappointments and crises by going directly to the nearest pub. Such joking sometimes seems a thin mask for a dedication to Aurelius's stoic noncomplaint.

Sir Thomas Browne.   Among the British influences on Grahame, one can point in particular to the works of Sir Thomas Browne, the mid-seventeenth-century physician and philosopher. Browne's religious mysticism is generally alien to Grahame's way of thinking, yet his apprehension of the natural world obviously appealed to Grahame. Browne says in *Religio Medici,* "There are two books from whence I collect my Divinity; besides the written one of God, is another of his servant Nature, that universal and publick manuscript, that lies expans'd unto the eyes of all."[4] While Grahame liked to think he had put the first book behind him, he certainly tried to read from the second.

Not only does Grahame quote from *Religio Medici, Pseudodoxia Epidemica (Vulgar Errors),* and *Hydriotaphia, Urn Burial*—frequently without citation—but Browne's method of exposition provides at times a structural model. Grahame learned somethng from Browne's idiosyncratic speculations on nature, his working out from concrete observed detail in many different lines of thought, although Grahame did not share the mystical turn that Browne's thoughts usually take. Grahame's first published essay, "By a Northern Furrow," is a good example of the kind of centrifugal development from the natural and concrete to the philosophical and speculative generally characteristic of Browne.[5] The stopping points in Grahame's movement outward are not those that Browne would have chosen, nor would Browne have attempted to return full circle to the concrete, as Grahame does, but structural likenesses exist nevertheless.

In this essay, the narrator establishes himself as an observer of a bare winter landscape, the Berkshire Downs in winter, where in the valley the marks of the plow are clearly outlined. As the narrator notes, he is, at first, tempted to allude to classical mythology, to associate the scene with Apollo, sentenced to plow behind the oxen of the sun. But then he finds this allusion inappropriate to the rigors of the northern winter and "the Scandinavian toilers of old time."[6] More appropriate, he muses, are the images evoked by painters of the Northern and Flemish schools. Their depiction of human suffering is "the enduring tie, the touch that kins us."[7] He remembers in particular a "Flemish Massacre of the Innocents," which he then describes in such vivid detail that anyone who has ever seen Brueghel's painting can identify it immediately. He moves on to consider Holbein's painting of the plowman, quoting Ruskin's analysis of it, which emphasizes the serenity and relief of death in such circumstances of endless toil. Serene depictions of death in lines from both Tennyson and Whitman then come to his mind. He considers also Pater's discussion of the superstitious clinging to life on the part of those who toil.[8] Finally, he pulls all of this speculation together by emphasizing that, in landscapes such as the one he is observing, the plow has paradoxical qualities. Not only does it prepare the earth to welcome new life, but, at the same time it turns up bits and pieces of skeletons, remnants of "three conquests." The history of this land and associations from literature and art all come together in a somewhat melancholy view of "a northern furrow."[9]

This essay is more serious and level in tone than those reprinted in *Pagan Papers* and displays more virtuosity in movement from thought to thought, although all these essays share rapid transitions. Sir Thomas Browne takes more daring theoretical leaps than Grahame and is less given to contemporary allusion, but the two essayists are alike in that their transitions in thought are rapid and associational rather than sequentially logical.

The romantic movement.   Like most of his contemporaries, Grahame was also an heir of romanticism in its philosophical as well as literary concerns. This statement could have many meanings, however; for in England by the late nineteenth century it is possible to trace at least two (and probably more) branchings out from the romantic movement, with shared dislikes, but with emphases so different that their common ancestry is easy to miss; they were certainly often at bitter odds.

As a convenient shorthand, one might designate the adherents of these two branches as the activists and the aesthetes. They generally shared a disdain for the technology of the industrial revolution, the excesses of Victorian puritanism, and the pettifogging concerns of the capitalist bourgeoisie. From these negative premises they go on to positive practices and beliefs that are often in opposition, despite their common ancestry. During the early 1890s, Grahame can be associated with both these branches, although he never dabbled in socialism, avoiding the Fabian Socialists; the latter were certainly less conservative than the activists, but considerably more activist than the aesthetes, with whom they had strong ties.

W. E. Henley, Grahame's first editor, epitomized the activist branch, which took off from Thomas Carlyle. Individualistic and agnostic, Henley was also politically conservative and imperialistic. His conservatism was, however, more feudal than capitalistic—harking back to a squirearchy and holding the landed gentry in higher esteem than the titans of industry. Like Henley, Grahame disdained the perceived hypocrisy of the established church, but was attracted to the landed establishment. His leanings in this direction are never as explicitly stated as Henley's. In his early essays, Grahame ignores or jokes about political matters. They are implicit in his fiction, particularly in *The Wind in the Willows*. Moreover, Grahame's individualism was quite different from Henley's. He would never have portrayed himself, as Henley did in "Invictus," with a "head bloody but unbowed." He was more likely to defend his right to idle the day away, as in his essay "Loafing."

This nonactivist strain in his individualism apparently attacted him to the prophets of the aesthetic movement—Ruskin, Pater, and Morris. Their advocacy of a life in art as both craft and appreciation, their emphasis on a closeness to nature and yearning for an agricultural past as a Golden Age, suited his temperament. His intense interest in Italian primitive painting seems to have been directly stimulated by them.

Where aestheticism led into a kind of bohemianism as it was then defined, Grahame could follow—at least in inclination—as his essay "A Bohemian in Exile" makes clear. Bohemianism in the English nineties meant, among other things, a "dropping out" from the demands of the workaday world in favor of a romanticized gypsy existence, living in a horsedrawn caravan, abandoning ties and property.[10] It also meant taking along, according to Grahame, "a few canvases and other artists' materials; soda-water, whiskey, and such like necessaries" (*P*, 77). Characteristically, Grahame could joke here in this early work about a life-style that attracted him, although the idea of a man's possible disappearance from his everyday world haunts him, arising again in "Orion" and two other essays, "The Long Odds" and "The Iniquity of Oblivion," both of which appeared in the *Yellow*

Book in 1895. Another aspect of bohemianism, its association with sexual freedom and unconventionality, Grahame tended to ignore. The extremes of the aesthetic movement that embraced what Henley and others considered "decadence," and, in particular, sexual experimentation, Grahame shunned.

By the 1890s and in the wake of the Victorian sentimentality with regard to family, the original romantic ideas of the child as superior in perception to the man, so apparent in the works of Wordsworth and Blake, had degenerated into a sloppy image of childish innocence. One of Grahame's prime contributions in *The Golden Age* and *Dream Days* was to restore the image of the perceptive child to its romantic beginnings, while adding to it a certain sharpness of understanding of the conflictual nature of childhood, brought out previously perhaps only by a few of the great realistic novelists of the nineteenth century.[11] The last six pieces of *Pagan Papers,* later to be printed elsewhere, are the beginnings of Grahame's exploration of childhood, based to some extent on romantic ideals.

Neo-paganism.   Perhaps also a corruption and certainly an extension of certain romantic ideals was a kind of neo-paganism that came to a head in the nineties in some extreme forms.[12] The sense of the high value of a communion with nature, expressed in Wordsworth's *Prelude* and already threatened there by urbanism, had by Grahame's time become a looming concern. A pervasive fin de siècle anxiety reigned among British intellectuals, characterized by a gnawing disappointment and frustration with the results of industrialization and a sense of alienation from one's "natural" state of being, an alienation generally attributed to restraints placed upon "the natural man" by Victorian society and religion.

This neo-paganism, while negative in reaction to the established churches, was not a religious movement but a literary one—much like pastoralism to which it was akin in many ways, including its nostalgia for an imagined ideal past. Characteristic of this neo-paganism was an animism in relation to nature. The image of the flute-playing Pan, half animal, half artistic man, was particularly appealing. Pan became emblematic of communion and direct connection with the world of nature both inside and outside themselves from which these men of the nineties—and clearly Grahame among them—felt divided by circumstances largely beyond their control.[13] In this variety of dualism, the emotional and physical self, as opposed to the intellectual, socialized self, is conceived to belong to the natural animal world. Grahame, however, accepts only part of the pervasive myth of Pan—as benign protector of natural creatures—while generally ignoring his brutal sexuality, an aspect emphasized by many of Grahame's contemporaries.[14]

In *Pagan Papers*, three essays display this neo-paganism: "The Rural Pan," "The Lost Centaur," and "Orion." The first of these takes its name from Matthew Arnold's "Lines Written in Kensington Garden," the first stanza of which Grahame copied down early in his bank ledger:

> In the huge world that roars hard by,
> Be others happy if they can.
> But in my helpless cradle I
> Was breathed on by the rural Pan.

Arnold's stanza opposes the bustle of the workaday world to the peace of the rural world of Pan. Throughout Grahame's piece, the narrator personifies his fellowmen as either Mercuries (mercantile men) or Apollos (dandies) who pursue vigorous leisure-time activities in groups that keep them from ever meeting that other god, Pan. For Pan haunts secluded streams, woods, and footpaths and, when the weather is rough, mingles with "unpretentious humankind" in a "sheltering inn" imparting "strange lore and quaint fancy" (*P, 37*). All of the various disapproved and approved activities are described whimsically and Pan himself seems hardly awesome but jolly and benign. The characteristic note of warning, however, is struck at the end, when the narrator points to the "growing tyranny" of the "iron horse" that brings commercialism, driving "the kindly god the well wisher to man—whither?" (*P, 38*). This juxtaposition of the railway and the rural countryside is a familiar topos of nineteenth-century pastoral literature.[15] The anxiety about encroaching technological change and urbanization is not original, but the depiction of Pan as the benign, social creature is for the most part Grahame's own creation—kin to the fatherly Pan he creates in *The Wind in the Willows;* it is not the Pan of his contemporaries.

Both "The Lost Centaur' and "Orion" come closer to expressing the serious aspects of neo-paganism of Grahame's time. The former adopts an elegiac tone and refers to the "wise and kindly" Cheiron, half man, half horse, who supposedly nurtured Achilles. It mourns a lost relationship with animal kind that human children ever try to

renew and from which they are eventually weaned. The narrator explicitly denies any wish to return to "The Goat Foot" (Pan), whom
he describes in this essay (in contrast to "The Rural Pan") as "peevish
and irascible" (*P*, 102). He claims, however, to discern a "mute and
stunted human embryo" gazing appealingly out of animals' eyes, re-
proaching humans for the "lamentable cleavage" brought about by
the "long race after . . . so-called progress." Had humans and animals stayed closer perhaps there might have been "some perfect embodiment of the dual nature: as who should say a being with the
nobilities of both of us, the baseness of neither" (*P*, 103). This essay
sees that opportunity for oneness as "long since lost."

In "Orion," the narrator begins by looking up at a night sky and
seeing the two constellations, the Plow and the Hunter; the latter is
Orion, whom he depicts as having long been driven from earth by
the men of the plow. Nevertheless, the narrator speculates, the
hunter still resides in all of us—as a wild streak, called by some
"Original Sin," which he here celebrates as an adventurous virtue,
rather than a vice, in children and a few others. The hunter is difficult to follow in modern times, yet, as the narrator notes, he does
still rise to take over the sky—and may let loose his arrow again. Unlike some of his contemporaries, however, Grahame was unwilling to
explore further in direct thought or action his perception of the "drop
of primal quicksilver in the blood" that he postulates in "Orion."[16]

The Informal Essay and Grahame's Predecessors, Stevenson and Jefferies

The informal essay form to which Grahame's early works belong,
while not stemming from ancient tradition, had, by Grahame's time,
some three hundred years of tradition behind it, traced, as is customary, back to Montaigne's *Essais* of 1580. These relatively short prose
works are generally characterized by an air of "tentativeness," which
is why Montaigne called them "attempts." They were never meant to
be definitive, but still were likely to approach serious philosophical
and ethical topics in personal, occasionally idiosyncratic, ways. Montaigne is reputed to have said, "Myself am the groundwork of my
book."[17]

The personal element in such essays is not emotionally "confessional" but more generally intellectual. As one commentator on Sir
Thomas Browne put it, in a personal essay one feels the "presence of

an individual mind thinking on a subject" subjecting "received truths to personal observation, experience, and reason in a kinetic form that emphasizes the process as much as its content."[18] As the essay developed in England, especially as it began to appear in periodicals, it often became political or satirical, or else evinced a certain levity or lightness of tone. Grahame tended toward this levity, adopting, as has already been suggested, a joking, almost bantering, tone toward topics that he seemed, nevertheless, to take rather seriously. This levity then seems a defense that adds a note of ironic self-reflexion to his personal essay style.

Grahame and R. L. Stevenson.   When *Pagan Papers* first appeared, Grahame's essays were considered derivative by some reviewers. One characterized them unflatteringly as "Stevensonettes," suggesting not only Grahame's excessive debt to R. L. Stevenson but a certain trivializing of Stevenson's thought as it appeared in collections of essays such as *Virginibus Puerisque* (1881).[19] An examination of the latter and *Pagan Papers* side by side and a comparison of essays on similar topics, such as Stevenson's "An Apology for Idlers," "Walking Tours," and "Pan's Pipes" with Grahame's "Loafing," "Romance of the Road," and "The Rural Pan," respectively, reveal many common subjects. These are, however, often found in the works of earlier essayists as well, for instance Montaigne's "On Idleness," or Hazlitt's "On Going on a Journey," to which Stevenson refers in his "Walking Tours." Stevenson's treatment of these topics does not appear universally or patently superior to Grahame's, but comparison does reveal important differences in form and content worth noting because they increase our understanding of strengths and weaknesses in Grahame's writing beyond *Pagan Papers*.

One of the first noticeable differences is that Grahame's pieces are shorter than Stevenson's and less didactic or serious in tone. For example, the notion of an "apology" with its need to justify "idleness," governs the length and rhetorical stance of Stevenson's essay.[20] Addressing the reader directly as "you," he is setting out here to prove through reasonable demonstration that idleness (even when, seen from the outside, it appears precisely like Grahame's "loafing") is not really idleness, but the seizing of an opportunity to learn lessons other than those learned in school or business. Stevenson advocates this way of life, generally by argument, but once by the depiction of a stiffly personified conversation between Mr. Worldly Wiseman and an Idler.[21] Stevenson's idler is really busy acquiring "knowledge of life at large, and Art of Living." He will become wise and "will not be heard among the dogmatists."[22]

Grahame talks of loafing not as a way of life but as a choice of holiday occupation in contrast to vigorous activities. The narrator justifies loafing in one sentence by saying that "action, indeed, is only the means to an end of reflection and appreciation" (P, 22). He assumes, unlike Stevenson—perhaps because Stevenson and others had done the arguing before him—that "reflection and appreciation" are held generally to be good. His loafer is, therefore, good because he seeks these ends directly, not bothering with action. The narrator notes the sly pleasure the loafer gets from contemplating others' activities: "it is chiefly by keeping ever in view the struggles and clamorous jostlings of the unenlightened making holiday that he is able to realize the bliss of his own condition and maintain his self-satisfaction at a boiling point" (P, 23).

The major portion of this essay is, however, an account of the loafer's day from leisurely breakfast to sound sleep. In its course this lucky man exchanges civilities with village dogs, smokes, lies in meadows, drinks beer, and paddles quietly in a boat, noticing the beauties of nature, master of all he surveys; "The loosestrife is his, and the arrowhead: his the distant moan of the weir; his are the glories, amber and scarlet and silver, of the sunset-haunted surface" (P, 28). The rewards of such relaxed mastery are generally sensuous. The reader is invited to experience the leisurely mood of the loafer's day. Grahame convinces not by argument but by evocation. This characteristic can be seen as either strength or weakness. The fluctuation in tone between the bantering of the first passage noted above and the seriousness of the second, with its biblical cadences, may also be seen variously.[23] Stevenson certainly keeps a more level earnest tone and never sinks to banter nor rises to sensuous ecstacy.

Unlike Stevenson's essays, Grahame's are grounded in space and sometimes in time. In this regard, one should note a statement in Stevenson's "Walking Tours" that could never have been made by Grahame: "But landscape on a walking tour is quite accessory. He who is of the brotherhood does not voyage in quest of the picturesque. . . ."[24] Grahame's "Romance of the Road" seems almost a response to Stevenson. Grahame is concerned in particular detail with the North Berkshire Downs Ridgeway and expresses its "pleasant personality," evoking not only past events along this old Roman road, but also evocative sights the walker might today see. Although he recalls the pleasure of the starting out and the contentment of completion, in contrast to Stevenson, Grahame calls on us to savor "All that lay between!" (*P, 5*).

This essay, like most of Grahame's essays, seems to be moving toward his fiction, and here specifically toward *The Wind in the Willows,* where setting becomes almost as important as character. A movement toward fictionalized character appears as well in Grahame's narrative voice, which is more personalized than the voice in Stevenson's essays. Also, the personalities we meet in Grahame's essays are never pure personifications as, for example, Stevenson's "Mr. Worldly Wiseman"; their conversation is always colloquial rather than formal.

Stevenson does not soften the myth of Pan. In "Pan's Pipes," Stevenson discusses the changeability of nature and emphasizes its dangerous and frightening aspects, using Pan and his music as an emblem of nature's paradoxical qualities.[25] He carefully develops a sense of what it means to "panic" and how this active terror relates to rites of the ancient God. Grahame's jovial God of "The Rural Pan" would certainly never fill his followers with panic. Grahame's brief mention of Pan as the Goatfoot in "The Lost Centaur" is much more like Stevenson's vision, however; "Orion" indeed seems to challenge and flirt with forces that Stevenson so carefully analyzes and against which he attempts to arm his reader.

Stevenson and Grahame thus seem to cover much common ground and this discussion does not exhaust their shared topics. Another essay of Stevenson's in the same volume, "Child's Play," will be considered in relation to *The Golden Age* and *Dream Days,* and Stevenson's adventure stories, *Treasure Island* and *Kidnapped,* examined in relation to Grahame's quite different writing for children. All these studies will suggest much the same thing, nevertheless: that differences in style and structure indicate great differences in the minds and imaginations through which common concerns are filtered.

Grahame and Richard Jefferies. Contemporary reviewers seemed not as aware of another possible influence on Grahame, that of Richard Jefferies. Relatively unknown today, although not without followers still, Jefferies struggled through poverty and illness in his brief life (1848–87) to pull himself up by the bootstraps from farmer's son to man of letters. His best known adult novels are *After London* (1885) and *Amaryllis at the Fair* (1887), but a cluster of works published in the early eighties are of concern here. In them, Jefferies generally makes use of the Wiltshire setting of his boyhood, very similar to the Downs of Berkshire about which Grahame wrote. These are *Wood Magic* (1881), *Bevis: The Story of a Boy* (1882), *Nature Near London* (1883), and *The Story of My Heart* (1883). An examination of *The Story of My Heart* in particular can cast light on that very quality in Grahame's essays that distinguishes him most clearly from Stevenson.

Jefferies's contemplation of nature, like Sir Thomas Browne's, is a profoundly absorbed one; like Browne, he attempts to "read" nature, but unlike Browne, does not attempt to decipher in it a message sent from God. Jefferies is not amystical, but his mysticism is not metaphysical: the experience of nature, at least in *The Story of My Heart,* is complete, total, and all-consuming in itself, both physical and spiritual. Jefferies absorbs himself in a specific setting and makes himself at one with it. The chapters of *Nature Near London* seem relatively conventional if sharply delineated nature essays, far more wholeheartedly dedicated to observation than Grahame's (and, they probably influenced Grahame's description of the river in *The Wind in the Willows*). His writing in *The Story of My Heart* is, in contrast, not the short essay form suitable for publication in periodicals. Jefferies's book is like extended continuous musing, broken into chapters; it is leisurely, repetitive, hypnotic, confessional, and meditative. As Peter Green puts it, "Jefferies practiced a passionate communion with earth and sun and sky."[26] Jefferies, like many of Grahame's fellow writers in the romantic tradition, was antipuritan and disturbed by the encroachments of urbanism on the countryside and rural way of life, finding both puritanism and urbanism equally blunting to individual sensation and experience. Since this type of thinking was fairly widespread at the time, Jefferies's particular influence on Grahame would not be noteworthy if there were not some important likenesses in their writing, accompanied by some equally important differences.

Strikingly similar passages appear in Grahame's "Loafing" (*P,* 27) and Jefferies's *The Story of My Heart*. Grahame shows his loafer "alone with south-west wind and the blue sky. . . . Prone on his back on the springy turf, gazing up into the sky." Jefferies says, "I was utterly alone with the Sun and the earth. Sometimes lying down on the sward I just looked up at the sky, gazing for a long time till I could see deep into the azure. . . ." Both experience transcendence into another state of being. "The fleshy integument" of Grahame's loafer, "seems to drop away and the spirit ranges at will among the tranquil clouds." Jefferies describes it thus: "I now became lost and absorbed into the being or existence of the universe."[27]

But Grahame's loafer and Jefferies "I" actually move in very different directions from each other. The loafer's experience is one of *freedom through separation:* "Earth no longer obtrudes herself. . . . His is now an astral body, and through golden spaces of imagination his soul is winging her untrammelled flight." Jefferies's experience is one of mystic integration: "I felt deep down into the earth under and high above into the sky and farther still to the sun and stars. Still farther beyond the stars into the hollow of space, and losing thus my separateness of being came to seem like a part of the whole."[28]

These differences again reveal Grahame's individuality in its strengths and weaknesses. Using the third person to distance narrative voice from "the Loafer," Grahame proceeds to describe an experience of separation on the Loafer's part, first from "sordid humanity" and then from his own "fleshy integument" and earthly concerns, in order to achieve the abstract level of imagination, a state of being distinguished by lack of boundaries ("golden spaces") and ties ("untrammelled flight"). Neither Grahame nor his creation, the loafer, can sustain this free floating vision; the lines that immediately follow are "And there he might remain forever, but that his vagrom spirit is called back to earth by a gentle but resistless, very human summons—a gradual, consuming Pantegruelian, god-like thirst. . . ." Off he trots to the nearest pub, an interruption justified by these mock-serious lines: "Tobacco for one is good; to commune with himself and be still is truest wisdom; but beer is a thing of deity—beer is divine" (*P,* 28).

Not so with Jefferies; the lines quoted are culled from recurring experiences, each described in detail, in which the "I" actively and deliberately attempts to participate in an experience, not escape from it. Jefferies cultivates meditation. At the point, for instance, when Jefferies is "utterly alone with the sun and the earth and the distant sea," he attempts successively to communciate with each—experiencing an "emotion of the soul" that he can only describe as prayer, although "prayer is a puny thing to it."[29] For Jefferies, as for most mystics, to lose oneself is to find oneself in something greater than oneself. This is a different level of freedom from that for which Grahame longs. Jefferies is not always able to sustain such a state, but he would never dilute it with beer.[30]

In contrast to Jefferies, Grahame can appear a mere dabbler in the experience of communion with nature. Yet, in spite of Grahame's variability in tone, his attraction to the idea of such a communion is apparent, especially if such communion will allow him to escape from both a frustrating world and a self that more clearly than Jefferies has lent itself to that world.

Not only Jefferies's detailed nature descriptions but the anthropomorphism of *Wood Magic,* where Jefferies depicts talking animals and birds, as well as a talking river and wind, are echoed in Grahame's writing. Moreover, Jefferies's depictions of young boys as complicated creatures, sensitive to nature, goes into Grahame's conception of the child. Writers do not, after all, build their imaginations on their own immediate experience alone, but also on the imaginations that appeal to them in the works of others. At some profound level, Jefferies seems to have helped form the filter through which Grahame's own experiences of nature and of childhood passed before they became a part of his art. The problem of tone, however, in essays like "Loafing" (although far less in "By a Northern Furrow,") makes us take Grahame's experiences of nature as superficial when compared to Jefferies's; yet these experiences still seem evocative and not trivial when compared to Stevenson's seeming blindness to natural setting.

Escapist Themes in *Pagan Papers*

Two of Grahame's modern biographers call our attention to one major theme in *Pagan Papers*. Eleanor Graham remarks that all of the essays, except those in "The Golden Age" section, emphasize a particular type of escape, "not adventurous escape, but avoidance rather."[31] In this line, Peter Green points out that much writing of this period, Grahame's included, features certain stock subjects, viewed in a certain stock way: "food and drink, tobacco, sleep, travel, walking, nature-mysticism and the rest of them . . . are all regarded as *drugs,* either stimulant or soporific, escape routes from an intolerable everyday reality."[32] On the whole, Green finds Grahame measured rather than excessive in this regard, when compared to many of his contemporaries.[33] He sees Grahame's variability in tone as a positive and commendable deterrent to such excesses.

"The intolerable everyday reality." Even when the tone is lightest, negative emotions are discernible in *Pagan Papers*. Grahame's negativism ranges from mild annoyance through a generalized sense of distress to a deep and personal anger at the exigencies of everyday reality.

Perhaps in the first category are the snobbish slurs he makes on the pretensions of the lower classes to culture in "Cheap Knowledge," in which he argues against free libraries where "every lad and lass can enter and call for Miss Braddon and batten thereon 'in luxury's sofa-lap of leather' " (*P*, 30). Annoyance merging into both distress and anger is also expressed in "Deus Terminus," where modern life is depicted as a life full of unnecessary boundaries, marking off first the countryside into particular properties, thereby destroying the "old enchantment" of the woodlands (described not in terms of natural beauties but chivalric romance), and then putting everyone into his or her proper work slot so that "the useless race of poets is fast dying out," while a kind of vulgar "Americanism" is rapidly coming in (*P*, 54). Grahame here suggests that railway stations are "the shrieking sulphureous houses of damnation erected as temples" to the God of Boundaries, that is, Deus Terminus (*P*, 55). Even clearer anger against modern encroachments on the countryside is expressed at the end of "The Rural Pan," where the railroad is seen as "the Iron Horse," bringing "Commercialism whose God is Jerry, and who studs the hills with stucco and garrotes the streams with the girder" (*P*, 38).

In "Romance of the Rail," however, Grahame takes a more objective stance. He maintains a speculative thoughtfulness throughout and muses that "the romance of the steam engine is yet to be captured and expressed," suggesting rather prophetically that it will not be so expressed "until it too is a vanished regret" (*P*, 11). He notes that Emerson, whom he quotes at length, thinks that "'Nature loves the gliding train of cars," and so should poets (*P*, 12). Grahame finds that painters like Turner and Frith have succeeded in blending trains into the landscape or making them picturesque in other ways. Although steamboats are far more romantic to Grahame, he does admit to a certain "sentimental weakness for the night-piercing whistle," which often causes him to fantasize about taking a "phantom train" north (*P*, 13).[34] This particular essay, in its sustained serious tone, is not particularly characteristic of *Pagan Papers*.

Already considered, "The Lost Centaur" and "Orion," with their sense of disconnection from animal origins and fundamental drives, reflect the general distress that neo-paganism expresses. What seems to be a much more personal bitterness lies behind a relatively face-

tious facade in "The Fairy Wicket," "Aboard the Galley," and "Justifiable Homicide." In "The Fairy Wicket," the narrator rails against
designing women, who, in modern life—now that the true gate to
"Elf-land" (i.e., the fairy wicket) is closed—pretend to belong to the
fairy race and trick men into thinking that they can lead them to this
gate, leading them instead to "a cheap, suburban villa" (P, 92).

In "Aboard the Galley," the narrator bitterly compares the plight
of all modern men to that of dead and mummified men who, according to a certain native funeral rite, were put to the oars of funeral
ships and set out to sea: "all we . . . are but galley slaves of the basest
sort" (P, 94). While despairing of any real rebellion from this servile
state, the narrator fantasizes making certain prime offenders, "trai-
tors," walk the plank of this allegorical galley ship. Most of those
whom he would have walk the plank are of an annoying but trivial
nature, but the narrator makes more serious and bitter charges against
relatives, "who never believe in us, who know (and never forget) the
follies of our adolescence; who are always wanting us *not* to do things;
who are lavish of advice, yet angered by the faintest suggestion of a
small advance in cash: shall the idle singers perish and these endure?"
(P, 97). When, however, he tries to imagine a moment when all the
galley slaves might arise and, forgetting their differences, throw off
their masters, he is unable to do this. He can imagine them only
quarreling among themselves; characteristically, he finally opts for
law and order and the status quo over chaotic rebellion.

Relatives are again the butt of Grahame's facetiously disguised anger in "Justifiable Homicide." A young man, the narrator says,
should be able to arise and "deal with his relations" at whose mercy
he has been "during his minority" (P, 83). The narrator asserts that
in Afghanistan there is a code "that fully provides for relatives who
neglect or misunderstand their obligations" (P, 84). He then glee-
fully tells two stories of young nephews from those parts who have
taken full advantage of this code and dispatched uncles; one nephew
boasts, "I got him from behind a rock" (P, 86). The narrator also
remembers in England one of the "few of the old school" who used to
dispose of a relative every spring, greatly to his financial advantage—
although he did it as a duty. Unfortunately, after a long and successful career of such "justifiable homicide," he was caught and there
were, as the narrator aptly puts it, "few relatives to mourn his un-
timely end" (P, 87).

Grahame's outrageous suggestions might be compared with Jona-
than Swift's even more outrageous "A Modest Proposal" (1729). Swift

depends on an ironic flipflop in order to indict English policy in Ireland. When he suggests eating Irish babies, he clearly means to satirize others; no one was meant to take the proposal as serious (although some did), and the monstrous suggestion certainly does not reflect Swift's wishful thinking. Grahame depends on his audience to read in the same irony; yet one wonders whether wishful thinking is not also present! If "the final solution" is facetious, the sense of oppression and frustrated anger is heartfelt.

A little fragment of an unpublished essay, entitled "Plate Smashing and the Conjuror," also suggests Grahame's need for violent outburst and his perception of this need below the civilized facade. Interestingly enough he here uses a rather Freudian term, "subconscious ego" (comparable to the Id?) to designate the site of such a need. Grahame muses in this passage on the reasons why we are entertained by plate smashing in music halls or by magicians pulling rabbits out of silk hats. With regard to the former, he states, in a wonderful burst of language, that smashing of plates affords an emotional release: "It must be an extravagant abuse of plates; a cataclysm of plates; a cataract of plates dancing from dresser or table; an unimaginable holocaust of plates. . . ." This pent-up emotion, he notes, could just as well be tears as laughter, except that everyone in the audience is well fed and comfortably seated, expecting to laugh. In the image of his contented audience, he reminds us of constraints attractive to him, but earlier in the passage he has mentioned the seriousness of breaking even one plate, "in your rich uncle's collection."[35] The latter is a constraint that no doubt gives an angry personal thrust to the pleasurable release of a "holocaust of plates."[36]

In "The Eternal Whither," Grahame contemplates holiday pastimes, as he often does. Here, however, are two unusual ones for the weary business man. Having heard of two bank clerks, one of whom kept a tollgate in his spare time while the other indulged in horse stealing, the narrator opts for the second and suggests, "Why not try crime?" "These new pleasures . . . would furnish just the gentle stimulant, that peaceful sense of change so necessary to the tired worker" (P, 48). Of course, he notes, not everyone has the appropriate makeup for crime and could find other simple pleasures in taking tolls. "These for the weaker brethren," he says, "but for him who is conscious of the Gift, the path is plain" (P, 50). Again, the bank clerk *cum* essayist toys with the idea of forbidden violence rather than simple escape.

Not least of the routes of escape from "intolerable reality" for a writer may be to sublimate feelings of angry frustration into pieces like "Aboard the Galley," "Justifiable Homicide" and "The Eternal Whither" in which wishes for violent reaction are indirectly indulged. Usually Grahame takes the self-protective precaution of signaling that he is not serious about revenge by making all into an exaggerated joke.

The dilettantish escape. Consciously, Grahame gives the seal of approval to means of escape more conventional than killng off your tormentors but also easier than sublimation in writing. Dilettantish pastimes, in which one observes rather than labors or finds temporary pleasure in a specific indulgence, are not only the subject of "Loafing," but of "Non Libri Sed Liberi" and "Of Smoking." A curious essay, "Marginalia," also deserves notice in this regard.

The title "Non Libra Sed Liberi" takes its form from an old Roman's smitten remark on first catching sight of some British slaves: "Not English [non Angli] but Angels [Sed Angeli]" (P, 17). This piece is partly a diatribe against bookbinders who tend to keep rare books from their owners for intolerable periods, for books are after all, as the title states and the narrator insists, not really books but children. He waxes fulsome on the delights of pursuing ("resembling the familiar but inferior passion of love") (P, 16) and owning books: "Once possessed, books develop a personality: they take on a touch of human life" (P, 17).

"Of Smoking" extols the virtues of pipesmoking and discriminates finely among the various sensuous pleasure available to the smoker. The narrator compares the taste of the first pipe of the day to "the kiss of one's first love" (P, 57), but berates women for disliking the smell of tobacco. In this essay, he parodically considers two subtopics: "Of Smoking in Bed" and "Concerning Cigars." He comes out in favor of both, with certain reservations. The most serious reservation is the idea that if the perfect cigar were found too early, the smoker would have nothing henceforth to anticipate. The narrator considers, however, the possibility of further inexpensive research, sampling the cigars of friends; he notes that a young man, if he can't "live up to his father's income" can, at least, "resolutely smoke his father's cigars" (P, 62). Book collecting and smoking are clearly two absorbing pastimes that may be compared favorably to the "higher" passions—and both can be addictive.

At the end of "Marginalia," the narrator asks a prophetic question: "When shall that true poet arise who, disdaining the trivialities of text, shall give the world a book of verse consisting entirely of margin?" (*P*, 43–44). Here Grahame has been using the concept of wider and wider margins to comment upon the poetry of his contemporaries. Grahame's vision of the happy doddler, filling up margins, and especially the schoolboy escaping into margins where he draws marginalia both imaginative and rude, precedes his critical consideration of the length of the poetic line. The idea of a book filled entirely by blank pages may indeed at this time of Grahame's life have seemed mainly a challenge; later on it could have become a nightmare of unfulfilled promise.

Total escape.   Total escape in the form of running away from worldly concerns is, as already noted, the subject of "A Bohemian in Exile," where a friend of the narrator's, one Fothergill, takes off in a caravan. During the period when these essays were written, Henley was urging upon Grahame a complete commitment to the literary life. Noteworthy, however, is the fact that such a possibility is considered in none of the "escape" essays of the period, neither those in *Pagan Papers* nor those immediately following its publication. Published in 1895, both "The Iniquity of Oblivion" and "The Long Odds" play on the idea of a life alternative to the one in which Grahame found himself enmeshed, yet writing as a profession was apparently no obvious or desirable escape to Grahame. Fothergill, the "Bohemian," one senses, made more use of the whiskey and soda than of the canvases stacked in his caravan, yet died happy withal.

To understand both the depth of Grahame's longing for escape, even from the literary life, and the strength of the ties that bind Grahame to the life he would escape, one must examine "The Iniquity of Oblivion" and "The Long Odds" more closely. The former is obstensibly an essay about forgetting and how bad that is.[37] It begins with an inquiry about whether the reader has ever forgotten a dinner engagement. The narrator here disputes the likely immediate answer, "No," not only on the grounds of our obvious propensity to conceal such a social misdemeanor, but also by asking a question that becomes existential: if your host does not tell you, "How do you know?"[38] This leads him to speculate that perhaps we all lead lives of at least double, but mutually exclusive, consciousnesses. He postulates this on the fact that he, for instance, dreams in detail of a certain room he rented and furnished in London that he has never been able to find, no matter how he searched. He wonders, "was I all the time leading, somewhere, another life—a life within a life—a life that I constantly forgot, within the life that I happened to remember?"[39] This "life within a life" is clearly the more attractive. He goes on to tell the story of a certain man who "wore drab spats all the year around, lived in a suburb, and did daily business on the 'Baltic' [Exchange]." This man perhaps had such a "life within a life," for, in making periodic visits to the early Tuscan exhibit at the National Gallery, he usually disappeared from his everyday scene for a long period of time. Says the narrator, "I like to think that there was some bit of another life hidden away in him—some tranced memory of another far-away existence on Apennine Slopes."[40] The narrator then imagines that "far-away existence" in some detail. The essay concludes with a speculation on Oblivion's habit of swallowing up the good memories and leaving the humiliating ones. Analysis of "The Iniquity of Oblivion" suggests that the idea of an escape into an alternate life achieved through external or internal forces beyond one's conscious control was a particularly attractive one for Grahame.[41]

Still another drop-out from the halls of commerce is seen in "The Long Odds," where the narrator describes an elderly man whom he supposedly met in Venice, a virtual beachcomber.[42] This former Englishman had also been secretary of an august institution (one, no doubt, not unlike the Bank of England, where Grahame had in 1894 filled the post of acting secretary for a few months and was later to become secretary). This gentleman had, however, been so haunted by visions of board members past who died in their posts, checked off, as it were, by the blue pencil of Death, rather than the secretary's blue pencil (used to check the roll), that this erstwhile secretary had had himself pensioned off early (as Grahame was later to do) and gone south, where time seemed to him to stretch out pleasantly, rather than fly by.

This vignette of the beachcomber is enclosed in a discussion of how, when one is young, one wants adventure stories with enormous odds against the hero (with whom one identifies of course)—whole armies, which one is sure that the hero will defeat in the end, because he is the beloved of the gods. Later, the narrator points out, one becomes disillusioned with one's chances; no longer is one the favorite of the gods but the victim, so, like the beachcomber, one longs to drop out of the fray. Nevertheless, the narrator concludes, one cannot really drop out. Why? Because "from first to last fighting was the art we were always handiest at; and we are generally safe if we stick to it, whatever the foe, whatever the weapons—most of all whatever the cause."[43] Grahame does not make clear here just what vague but potent dangers he saw in not fighting the dubious fight that his job and life appeared to him.

Repeated in Grahame's essays is a vision of the South and particularly Italy as a perfect setting for escape.[44] This is partly because of its very contrast to England and northern Europe in general. In the literature of the period and even later, the mind-body, rational-irrational duality was frequently played out in terms of geography. One should remember, perhaps, in speculating about Grahame's unstated fears of ceasing to fight, not just his rather happy and harmless beachcomber of Venice, but also Aschenbach, the protagonist of Thomas Mann's *Death in Venice* (1911)—the epitome of what happens to the rational man of the North when he "escapes" to the irrational South. Chalmers has already drawn the analogy between "the respectable member of the Baltic Exchange" in the "Iniquity of Oblivion" and the Seafaring Rat in *The Wind in the Willows,* who tries to lure Ratty away from the River and almost succeeds.[45] In that case, Ratty is saved only by Mole's forcing him to return to his poetry—another suggestion of the sublimating role that literature played for Grahame, making the life he lived bearable, yet keeping him in it as well.

In "The Iniquity of Oblivion," forgetfulness in one mode of consciousness sometimes opened up another mode of consciousness—a rather attractive vision of forgotten happiness to which one might, periodically at least, escape. In "The White Poppy," a *Pagan Papers* essay, the narrator asks, while making a few jokes about creditors, for a different kind of forgetfulness, that perfect *blankness* brought about by the juice of the white poppy, "white as the stark death-shroud, pallid as the cheeks of that queen of a silent land whose temple she languorously crowns" (*P,* 68). Not an escape into a raised consciousness but one into a deadened consciousness, if not death itself, is what the narrator craves here.

Only in a few of the essays in *Pagan Papers* does Grahame fail to pull the reader back from seriousness of vision and inquiry by a deflating, self-reflexive comment. In "An Autumn Encounter" (*P,* 63–67), the narrator addresses a scarecrow seen as a "heartless mummer" taking on various guises as the hiker-narrator gets closer to him: a young girl walking toward his twenty-year-old self, a preacher taking on the eternally sinful crows, a faithless debonair lover, and finally the signpost to the nearest pub. Almost all of this piece operates on the light, deflationary level for, although its central image is that of the "hollow man" (who will later haunt T. S. Eliot as emblematic of modern man), only if one generally distrusts the true levity of Grahame's "joking" can one find ironic seriousness in this essay.

Grahame's persona.   The attempt to capture the essential "personality" of a personal essay often proves futile. Grahame's early essays in particular depend very much on the reader's mood and willingness to accept the narrator's point of view, riding the tide of its rapid changes in terms not only of what is being contemplated, but also of the level of seriousness with which it is being contemplated. With such acceptance, the reader experiences Grahame's ironic wit as part of this personality.

The choice of the personal essay form, however, also encourages the reader to identify the narrator with the author and to try, if one is so inclined, to understand both at a deeper level. Not only were Grahame's essays first published anonymously but, much like his social behavior, they are full of other distancing devices characteristic of neither Stevenson's argumentiveness nor Jefferies's meditativeness, for instance. His wit is only one of these distancing devices. More than either of these predecessors, Grahame creates a "persona," a special voice for his narrator, whose true nature and intent are hard to capture and analyze. The quality of these essays is elusive; their elusiveness seems a deliberate, not accidental quality that remains even after Grahame acknowledges his authorship.

The Later Essays

Five years after *The Wind in the Willows,* "The Fellow That Goes Alone" appeared in the Jubilee number of the *St. Edward's School Chronicle,* July 1913.[46] The piece begins with a legend about an Oxford saint, Edmund, who, as a boy walking by himself, was met by the Christ child, who said to him, "Hayle, felowe that goest alone." The narrator chooses to use this tale as an exemplum of the importance of walking alone, quite literally (not just allegorically), in order to meet not Christ, but your own freer self. On solitary hikes, the mind becomes "creative and suprasensitive, until at last it seems to be outside you and as it were talking to you while you are talking back to it." This is an "emancipation" "only attained in solitude."[47] In addition, if alone, the walker may be greeted by animals or birds as "a pal," if with others, as "a conspiracy"; in company one will lose the opportunity to have true adventures or indulge in "a touch of lunacy in action [that] will open magic doors to rare and unforgettable experiences."[48]

This essay may be seen as a key to Grahame's avoidance of intimacy and perhaps as emblematic of Grahame's particularly withdrawn and isolated state at the time, no longer creative, trapped in an inappropriate marriage and anxious about a troubled son. Certainly only the experience of isolated walking itself is important here to Grahame, for "not a fiftieth part of all your happy imaginings will you ever, later, recapture, note down, reduce to dull, inadequate words."[49] The theme of escape is still apparent, and Grahame has already been retired for five years in country and is, except in this instance, not writing.

In Rome, after Alastair's death, the Keats-Shelley Society prevailed upon Grahame to give their annual lecture. His talk, entitled "Ideals," was published in 1922.[50] The quality of this lecture is markedly different from that of most of Grahame's early essays. One notable aspect is the clear consciousness of an audience. The difficulty of assuming a literary "persona," distancing yourself from the voice of the work, is great in the lecture format and Grahame assumes a new distancing voice, that of the informal but polite lecturer. He opts for a quieter, more leisurely tone, emphasizing logical, expository organization reminiscent not of his own early essays, but of Stevenson's.

He explains that the "ideals" with which he is concerned are those longings for better things first expressed in a child's daydreams; he goes on to describe three classes of chidlren's daydreams: those about unknown places; those about unknown human beings; and those about objects that will come into their possession. Then he goes back and does the same for adults, reminding the audience of the various categories. Clarity is the chief trait of Grahame's plea for the continued existence of and necessity for daydream. Those daring leaps from association to association, however, are gone. Grahame himself suggests that he is here "almost preaching."[51]

Grahame begins his preface to the 1926 reissue of George Sanger's autobiography, *Seventy Years a Showman,* with the statement "Retirement and reminiscence are apt to trot in harness together. . . ."[52] He applies this to circus owner Sanger's writing, but it would apply equally well to Grahame's writing about "Sanger and His Times." For Grahame takes the opportunity to evoke the old-time traveling circuses and country fairs in detail, reminding us not of a sermon, but of Grahame's narrative skills. Into a review of Sanger's life and book,

Grahame weaves many strands: his own reminiscences of traveling circuses, alongside Sanger's; dissertations on various types of entertainment at country fairs, with special attention to merry-go-rounds and freak shows; thoughts about changes, both good and bad, in the country fair over the nineteenth and early twentieth centuries. The origins of the modern cinema in peep shows and lantern shows is a strand to be followed, along with references to Charles Dickens's interest in, and perception of, show people at the time that Sanger was developing his father's peep show into a fine spectacle.

Of note, too, is Grahame's insistence on the respectability of circus folk, differentiating them from Gypsies and emphasizing the cosiness of the caravan life they led, a picture of the traveling life that seems to have been held by Mr. Toad. But by 1926, Grahame also may have resigned himself for the most part to the many changes in everyday life that have taken place—including the changes from horse to motorcar. His nostalgia seems no longer tinged by a bitter longing for the pastoral scene. The excitement and glamour of London, as seen through the eyes of three circus sisters, is acknowledged.

Grahame's final image in this preface is not only characteristic of his lifelong enthusiasm for country rambling, but poignant, for a man who had too early lost both father and son. Speaking of George Sanger's triumphs, Grahame says, "For myself, I like best the early struggles, the simple joys and sorrows, the wanderings of little George and his indomitable father upon the open road with its alehouse and toll-gates, over commons, or with their pitch on a wayside strip of grass, with their peep-show and its accompanying patter."[53]

This introduction and Grahame's "Oxford Through a Boy's Eyes" are devoted to reminiscence and contemplation of permanence and change. In both, Grahame seems to have recaptured some of his old evocative powers. In "Oxford Through a Boy's Eyes," Grahame goes back sixty or so years to remember his boyhood arrival at Oxford Station, which he regards with mellow affection and not the scorn of "Deus Terminus."[54] Again the exuberant storyteller takes over: "Our hero then, still under the feminine control he was about to quit for the first time, was propelled into—what?—why a fly [one-horse covered cab] of course, for there was nothing else to be propelled into or by. All England at that period lay fly-blown under the sky, and flies crawled over its whole surface. Whatever station you arrived at, a fly crawled up to you and then crawled off with you."[55] The rest of the essay gives the impression indeed of an effort to see Oxford again through "a boy's eyes," to recapture some of the point of view not just of Kenneth at nine, but the younger writer Grahame of *The Golden Age* and *Dream Days*. It shifts back and forth from early impressions to late, to offer a sense of what has happened to Oxford (and Grahame) over the years.

What biographers have found most enlightening in this account is that, in addition to mentioning many of the sights that would have been attractive to most schoolboys, Grahame mentions his early habit of seeking admittance to, and strolling through, the walled gardens of Oxford, a horticultural taste not usually attributed to small boys. The shops of High Street with their goodies were a more normal schoolboy attraction and one that Grahame still admits to: "I love to roam its dusky and odorous corridors, gazing longingly at all the good things I'm no longer permitted to eat."[56]

The reminiscence that brought revival of evocative powers does not operate in "A Dark Star," a lecture delivered shortly before Grahame's death and also published posthumously.[57] Instead, we have what one might characterize, comparing it with "Ideals," as his late lecture style: lengthy, leisurely, orderly, attempting to make and carry a point. Both lectures mention the Socratic method—a key to Grahame's rhetorical model—although he does not actually provoke discussion.

The subject matter of this lecture is basically literary criticism. Grahame attempts to characterize a quality in some literary works that critics tend to ignore but which, like certain "dark," that is, invisible, stars, exerts an influence, attraction, or repulsion on surrounding objects. This force, visible only in its effect, must be taken into account in any judgment, contends Grahame. One might call it "contemporary appeal" or "incommunicable thrill." Only the contemporaries of the writer experience it; future generations of readers do not. In his own time, argues Grahame, the writer with such appeal achieves a higher rank in the minds of knowledgeable responsible readers than he will ever achieve later. Tennyson is here Grahame's prime example. He argues that this appeal is not true quality, yet is a formidable element not to be ignored; it accounts for many differences in critical analysis where one might expect agreement among reasonable men.

This essay implies that Grahame has been doing some scientific reading in his old age. He has become interested enough not only to use the analogy of the dark star, but is also familiar to some extent with the theory of relativity, for he applies some version of it to literature. Unlike many of his Victorian contemporaries, Grahame never appeared to participate in the great wave of amateur scientific investigation that swept England, sending many ladies and gentlemen out climbing hill and dale and shifting sand for "specimens." He certainly was no Beatrix Potter, observing every aspect of her animal friends scientifically before she made fictional characters of them. Thus, scientific analogy is a new element in Grahame's work and, since Grahame died shortly thereafter, a short-lived one.

One can view Grahame as pronouncing the last word on his mid-Victorian self as a writer in "A Dark Star." Yet the sense that we have a mind still vigorous—not simply mulling obsessively over the past and the same material, but beginning to measure it in ways fresh and new—makes this essay seem not simply an inadvertently ironic ending to Grahame's writing career. Still such irony would lie in our seeing "contemporary appeal" or "incommunicable thrill" as indeed the chief characteristic of most of Grahame's writing. One might well regard many of his essays in this light, but it will not adequately illumine the complexity of Grahame's fiction.

Chapter Three

Moving Toward Fiction: *The Headswoman* and Other Tales

Later incorporated into *The Golden Age,* the five stories that appeared at the end of the 1893 edition of *Pagan Papers* give the clearest indication of Grahame's move from the personal essay form into prose fiction, a move encouraged by his editor, W. E. Henley. Prior to this significant change in mode of presentation are other signs, both overt and subtle, of Grahame's movement toward fiction. The more subtle of these have to do with manipulations of point of view, even within the confines of the essay form. The essays considered here appeared about the same time as Grahame's early prose fiction.

The overt signs of Grahame's movement not just toward fiction, but toward fiction for children as well as adults, appear in the tales brought together in this chapter. They were written between 1890 and 1907 and belong together only in the sense that they are relatively short works of fiction, neither essays nor novels, and different from the stories of *The Golden Age* and *Dream Days* in both narrative stance and cast of characters. The first of this group of diverse tales, *The Headswoman,* stands out as being so different from the others that it finally represents a path *not* taken by Grahame—that of the satiric fable involving adult human beings. Like *The Golden Age* and *Dream Days, The Headswoman* is meant for an adult audience, but unlike them is concerned in no way with childhood. Also considered here are fables that Grahame makes up in his introductions and reviews; they begin to turn away from human beings as characters, are still directed at adult readers, yet show definite concern with childhood. Like *The Headswoman,* however, they sound a strong satiric note. Finally examined are two works often seen as "the first whispers of *The Wind in the Willows*": *The Reluctant Dragon* and "Bertie's Escapade."[1] Both are fantasies involving "animals" and clearly directed toward the child. These tales move away from direct social satire, but, like *The Wind in the Willows* itself, imply an adult as well as child reader.

Manipulations of Point of View

An interesting element to note in several of the essays of the 1890s is Grahame's tendency to force us to see human beings through the eyes of nonhuman beings or personifications. This tendency is related to the notion of seeing grown-ups through the eyes of children, as in *The Golden Age*, but here is more diffuse and somewhat paradoxical. For instance, two escape-oriented essays, both published in the *National Observer*, change point of view in the middle. "The Triton's Conch" begins by exalting the sea but ends with the sea god Triton personified, gazing wistfully at the pleasures of the earth.[2] "An Old Master" starts by exalting the sunny South, but also ends with a personification: the Sun, it seems, is waiting only for a little decorous worship from the British to come away from Italy and spend more time in England.[3] Here these changes of point of view have the effect of making escape by land or sea seem less necessary.

Two other essays center on the idea of animals' viewing humans with somewhat jaundiced eyes. In "The Inner Ear," published in the *Yellow Book* in 1895,[4] the narrator decries the degeneration of the human faculty of hearing when bombarded by "the clatter and roar of [London's] ceaseless wheels," and "the racket and din of a competitive striving humanity." Only early on a Sunday in the country does "that inner ear of ours [begin] to revive and record . . . the real facts of sound." These sounds range from the gossip of the rooks to "the very rush of sap, the thrust and foison of germination."[5] All these sounds, moreover, indicate "an entire indifference . . . towards ourselves, our conceits and our aspirations."[6] The narrator enumerates the ways in which insects and other beings "insult one at every turn by their bourgeois narrowness of non-recognition." Humans thus turn out to be "entirely superfluous"; or "awkward aliens, staggering pilgrims through a land whose customs and courtesies we never entirely mastered."[7]

In his introduction to Billinghurst's *A Hundred Fables of Aesop* (1899),[8] Grahame turns tables on human beings and tells two fables about them—tales purported to have come from a volume written by the beasts, who "feel and resent, very keenly indeed, the ungentlemanly manner in which they have been exploited, for moral purposes, by people with whom they only wished to live in mutual esteem and self respect."[9] The narrator (obviously a "persona") was allowed the great privilege of a "glimpse at the book one afternoon, in a pine wood, when the world was hot and sleepy, and the beasts had dined well."[10] The fables that he reads are considered specifically in the third section of this chapter.

In reading these pieces now, one may be reminded of what Grahame, in his *Pagan Papers* essay, "The Lost Centaur," says about the unfortunate separation of beasts and humans. Yet what is interestingly paradoxical about his use of the animals' point of view is that the narrator has never really abandoned his human stance and Grahame is still treating the creatures involved anthropomorphically; he is no more a naturalist than any other writer of fables. The turnaround in these pieces is not for the purposes of naturalism or realism, but for a mixture of somewhat whimsical fantasy and satire (on some occasions more disguised than others) of human folly and conceit. Although in *The Wind in the Willows* Grahame develops his animals more fully as characters, he certainly portrays them no more naturalistically there.[11]

Grahame cannot keep a slightly satirical note with regard to humankind's place in the universe from creeping into his favorable review of Evelyn Sharp's *All the Way to Fairyland* in 1899.[12] Here Grahame turns the tables again and suggests that we are all characters in a tale told by fairies, rather than the other way around: "Having pleased, in a whimsical moment to invent us (Lord only knows why), they have us at their mercy, and, as soon as they are tired of thinking of us, or want a new amusement—puff!—we shall go out and *that* story will be over."[13] He finds it fortunate that fairies, however, unlike humans "are loving, irrational and not easily wearied; and after all, humanity must possess many humorous points for the outsider that escape the encased observer within."[14]

The Headswoman

The satirical note sounds loud and clear in *The Headswoman*, a manuscript that Grahame apparently began in 1890, about the same time as women were first admitted to the Bank of England in clerical positions; it may be considered one of his first pieces of prose fiction.[15] This tale appeared in the *Yellow Book* in October 1894, about a year after the publication of *Pagan Papers* and a few months before *The Golden Age;* it was published as an unillustrated book of fifty-four pages in 1898.[16]

The Headswoman has received little critical attention. Contemporary reviewers considered it a story that effectively used and demolished arguments for women's rights. One can well read it as a satire on the bourgeois town fathers and as a work of gallows humor. The sixteenth-century setting, the satiric portrayal of the townspeople, the generally humanistic surface attitude toward Jeanne, as well as the gallows humor, suggest Voltaire's *Candide* as an important model for Grahame.[17] Read with a certain raised consciousness, however, this tale also resembles some of James Thurber's fables, not only in its use of a mythological setting, but in its underlying uneasiness about the prevailing relationships between men and women and implicit message about the potential dangerousness of women. Finally, perhaps, we have to go to *The Taming of the Shrew* for a similarly romantic solution to an incipient "war of the sexes."

Grahame's tale is set in the imaginary French town of St. Radegonde in the sixteenth century. It begins in the traditionally romantic month of May, when a most unromantic, but beautiful and articulate young woman, Jeanne, inherits by ancient right the job of executioner from her dead father. Appearing before the town council, she insists upon assuming the job, despite mild hints from the ineffectual Mayor that she might prefer not, and loud protests from a lower-class member of the council, Master Robinet, the tanner, who is compared in passing to Lewis Carroll's Bill-the-Lizard.[18] After she quite competently takes up her post (those who are beheaded obviously enjoy it), her cousin, Enguerrand, an incompetent lawyer, pleads with her to abandon it, not on the basis of his own material advantage (or so he claims since he would inherit the post) but of its being unladylike. He manages also to convey the message that she will become undesirable if she persists. Though she effectively demolishes his arguments, Jeanne is clearly affected by the last and takes the next day off with a headache—a move that rearouses M. Robinet's antifeminist protests in the town council. Upset by her cousin and incensed by M. Robinet's protests, conveyed to her by the mayor, Jeanne strolls out that evening and thus happens to meet the young and handsome Seigneur of the village, who has returned in disguise. They are clearly smitten with each other, but Jeanne withdraws from the unchaperoned situation.

The next day when, through a mix-up in the jail, the Seigneur, who has been on a drunken binge, is brought to her for execution, this mutual attraction does not stop Jeanne; she is the consummate craftswoman and likes to abide strictly by the rules. Unlike a contem-

poraneous creation, the Lord High Executioner in Gilbert and Sulli-
van's *Mikado,* who demurred when confronted with the reality of the
execution of Nanki-Poo, she prepared to do her best, with some mild
regret. Only in the nick of time is the Seigneur rescued by his men
from the ax. This gracious lord is filled with even more admiration
for Jeanne, and bearing no grudge, he invites her and the Mayor to
his Chateau. While the Mayor is berated by the old family retainer,
the Seigneur honorably courts Jeanne. The narrator says, "The official
seemed oozing out at her fingers and toes, while the woman's heart
beat even more distressingly" (*H,* 52). Jeanne is conquered; they
marry; she quits her job. Her cousin inherits the post and marries a
woman much more ladylike than Jeanne (he thinks). He never
achieves Jeanne's competence, but the whole town, nevertheless, lives
happily ever after.

On the surface level of this tale, one can be satisfied that the contemporary readers were wrong to see the women's movement as the
main object of satire. Jeanne proves herself to be perfectly reasonable
in her defense of women's right to work, just like some of the concerned women of his time whom Grahame admired.[19] Jeanne says,
" 'My motive, gentlemen, in demanding what is my due is a simple
one and (I trust) an honest one, and I desire that there should be no
misunderstanding. It is my wish to be dependent on no one. I am
both willing and able to work, and I only ask for what is the common
right of humanity—admission to the labour market . . .' " (*H,* 10).
Her claim to be the most qualified for the job is certainly proved true;
its form is a model of rational discourse, not often granted to females
by their satirists. Her cousin Enguerrand is depicted as both patently
self-interested and incompetent; the Mayor is a silly, obsequious man;
M. Robinet is a rude, prejudiced yokel; the Seigneur, while no fool,
does get himself into a drunken scrape.

Important, however, is the nature of the job in which Jeanne is so
competent and the way in which she is persuaded to quit it. As for
the first consideration, one might adopt the view that the choice of
profession for Jeanne is unconnected with any ideas about her sex and
simply serves as a vehicle for gallows humor and social satire on the
lust for cruel spectacle in the human race, as represented by the public execution. Such an interpretation seems to ignore a level of possibility consistent with Grahame's view of women in "The Fairy
Wicket," where they tempt men duplicitously into "suburban villas,"
or his later depiction of the powerful and emasculating bargewoman

in *The Wind in the Willows*. Jeanne is certainly able to make some cutting blows to the self-esteem of her cousin in the course of their talk, and the fact that he too is able to get at her, by denying love, may in this context be considered a good thing, since it certainly softens her up for the Seigneur. Had she not been turned away from her profession by the Seigneur's offer of marriage, "her round graceful arms" which "showed snowily against her dark blue skirt and scarlet tight-fitting bodice" (*H*, 32) might have eventually been transformed into the "big mottled arm[s]" of the bargewoman who throws Toad so unceremoniously into the river in chapter 10 of *The Wind in the Willows*. Fortunately for Jeanne as woman, *The Headswoman* suggests, the Seigneur discerns and is able to appeal to her womanly, nonofficial self.

While Petruchio in Shakespeare's *The Taming of the Shrew* had, indeed, to deal with a much more frenzied Kate, and used more drastic methods, both works make clear that the true way to tame a domineering woman (who, of course, *must* be tamed) is to get her where she can do no damage to others by loving her and marrying her. Both Petruchio and the Seigneur demand kisses of their newly subdued ladies, and the ladies are quite happy about that. In both cases the benefits that accrue to the men in recognizing and taming the power of dominant women will not accrue to their fellows who marry seemingly mild women like Kate's sister, Bianca, or Enguerrand's Clairette. These mild women do not reveal the apparently universal female desire to dominate until *after* the wedding. As for Enguerrand, "Rumor had it, that he had found his match and something over" (*H*, 53). The war of the sexes cannot be avoided, both works seem to say, but when men are aware of their opponents' lust for power, they can sometimes subdue it. It pays, of course, to be either as tough and sly as Petruchio, or a powerful and attractive lord like the Seigneur. Otherwise, one may end up like the Grahame's hen-pecked gentleman in *Dream Days* who escapes for the afternoon from his wife (and the curate) by taking two truant boys to the circus.

The sensuality of Jeanne and the Seigneur's encounter on the scaffold, where she devests him of his doublet and turns back the collar of his shirt (after which he kisses her fingers), can also suggest a deeper, more explicitly sexual level to the notion of a headswoman. Certainly other English writers of the 1890s, before Freud's revelations, play on fears of castration in the metaphor of beheading. In 1892, Wilde's *Salome* appeared in France; the English translation ap-

peared in 1894. Beardsley's illustration expressed male fears of powerful, sexual women. And sexual desire itself is made an agency of the
state and a punishing society in *The Headswoman,* where men "lose
their heads" willingly, mounting Jeanne's scaffold and laying themselves down on the block. This idea and the idea that women, in their
other "accepted" role, as maternal beings, are society's agents in the
taming and virtual emasculating of boys and men deserve more examination in Grahame's work as a whole than they have hitherto received.

Occasional Fables

The two fables created by Grahame for his introduction to Billinghurst's *A Hundred Fables of Aesop* supposedly come from a book of fables about humans written by animals in retaliation for the falsity of
the tales which men have perpetrated about them.[20] Their context—
a scene where the narrator is admitted one day to the company of
talking beasts in a pine woods—could easily catch a child's fancy, but
the fables are clearly directed at adults and might well have been
written by children in retaliation against parents, as by animals
against human beings.

The first, "The Ape and the Child in the Leghorn Hat," begins
like the traditional cautionary tale in which a naughty child naturally
gets punished for bad behavior. But the incident is seen through the
eyes of a monkey peer of the frolicsome ape "who in much careless
ease inhabited a lordly mansion in Regent's Park [zoo]." This ape,
doing what comes naturally, bites the finger of a child who, reluc-
tantly, at the urging of her mother, offers him her bun. "Her large
fat mother" is the culprit here, for she has "ordered her to observe
the pitty ickle monkey, so mild and gentle, and give it a piece of her
bun at once, like a good, kind charitable ickle girl."[21] After the child
is bitten, the mother shakes and cuffs her "unmercifully, protesting
that of all the naughty, tiresome self-willed trollops, and that never,
never, never would she take her a-pleasuring again." The moral is
ironically complex suggesting that—although "the human species
have an altogether singular and unaccountable method of rearing their
young"—these same children somehow grow up to be good citizens
and therefore animals should not think *they* know everything.[22]

The second tale is similar. In "The Dog, the Child and the Moon,"
a child "crying for the moon" is joined in the nursery by a dog howl-

ing for the moon. The mother, on entering, "smacked the child soundly for its folly and unreasonableness" but "patted and praised the dog. . . ." The animals' moral is this: "You can never tell with exactness how human beings will act, under any conditions"—so you might as well go ahead and do something forbidden if you really want to.[23]

Grahame returns to the fanciful context of the animal gathering, without comment on the content of these fables, but upon closer examination the two tales seem even more hostile than *The Golden Age* and *Dream Days* in their attitude toward Olympians. The fables are not concerned about human offenses toward animals but rather false sentimentality toward animals, and adult—particularly maternal—abuses of children.

Compared to these fables, the story that Grahame makes up for his review (1899) of H. DeVere Stacpoole's *Pierrette* (a book of tales "which are not really fairy tales . . . but rather the sort of stories that fairies tell each other—about mortals, of course"), seems nostalgic rather than bitter.[24] Grahame gives a fanciful history of the animals emerging from Noah's ark and proceeding to set up rules for the creation of dove-cots, toy arks, and other playthings, games, traditional sweets, as well as of fairy stories. This review is notable for its evocative details, particularly in descriptions of children's toys, for the animals decree that "cotton-wool smoke should forever puff cloudily out of wooden locomotives." They are responsible too for inserting "wonderful red and blue threads inside glass marbles" and many other delightful inventions. Grahame, indeed, seems never to have forgotten the kind of details that fascinate children and have a Proustian evocativeness for adults.[25] Unlike most adults, however, he seems not to have changed very much his own playthings. At the time of writing this piece, Grahame was amassing a collection of toys that later dominated his study.

The Reluctant Dragon

"A dragon," says Grahame, in a much-quoted passage from his introduction to Billinghurst's *A Hundred Fables of Aesop,* "is a more enduring animal than a pterodactyl. I have never yet met anyone who really believed in a pterodactyl; but every honest person believes in dragons—down in the back-kitchen of his consciousness."[26]

Grahame's only dragon story, *The Reluctant Dragon,* first appeared

as a story within a story in *Dream Days,* but has subsequently been
published, out of its original context, as an illustrated book for children.[27] The tale reads well on its own and, unlike *The Wind in the
Willows,* has a human child protagonist with whom the child reader
can immediately identify. Even a small child might easily relate to
the Boy, who is the rather bookish son of a shepherd and his wife,
unusual model parents in Grahame's world: "he was left to go his own
way and read as much as he liked; and instead of frequently getting
a cuff on the side of the head, as might well have happened to him,
he was treated more or less as an equal by his parents, who sensibly
thought it a very fair division of labour that they should supply the
practical knowledge and he the booklearning" (*D,* 157).

One night, the shepherd returns home, disturbed, to report a great
scaly creature snoring near a cave on the Downs. The Boy identifies
the beast immediately as a dragon and suggests that the next day after
tea he should go to negotiate with him—a solution that puts his ami-
able parents' minds at ease. Indeed, on further acquaintance, the
Dragon turns out to be a lazy, peaceable chap, who has escaped ex-
tinction (suggesting he is as much a pterodactyl as a dragon) by bur-
rowing down into the earth and amusing himself through the eons
composing poetry, with which he would be pleased to entertain the
boy. They strike up a mutually satisfying friendship, interrupted by
the arrival of St. George in town, drawn hither by the tall tales of
the villagers about the violent exploits of their resident dragon. The
Boy warns the Dragon of the probable conflict, but the latter insists
on leaving everything up to the Boy to avoid a fight.

When approached, St. George is persuaded by the Boy that the
Dragon is a peaceful fellow, but the Saint insists that a fight must be
arranged to satisfy tradition. The three meet and decide on a mock
battle during which the Dragon will be vanquished by a blow in a
nonvulnerable spot; he will subsequently be "reformed" rather than
executed by St. George. The Dragon has sold himself on this idea,
anticipating the traditional banquet to follow the fight, a banquet at
which he plans to make his social debut. On the day of the fight, the
Dragon proves himself to be a fine showman, but, as planned, is defeated in three rounds. The banquet goes off as planned, too, with the
Dragon the hit of the evening. The story ends with the Boy having to
seek assistance from St. George to escort the Dragon, rather the worse
for drink, back to his lair. The three friends then "set off up the hill
arm-in-arm, the Saint, the Dragon and the Boy" (*D,* 201).

Model for a number of future dragon stories for children that break with stereotypical traditions about the archetypal beasts, this story is also particularly successful at exploiting the tradition for what it is worth. Grahame manages to give the child satisfying control over the adult situation and to make him a hero in peacemaking. The Boy also has an opportunity safely to express annoyance with and anger at frustrating adult behavior, calling the Dragon in his drunkenness "a great lumbering *pig*," for instance (*D*, 200). Nor is all glamor and drama lost, for the fight itself is a fine spectacle, just as it was meant to be in the heroic tradition—with the Dragon's turquoise scales and St. George's gold armor gleaming in the sun.

Grahame treats neither mythological creatures nor real animals naturalistically. Had the Dragon been a pterodactyl he would have been just as anthropomorphic. Upon examination, the Dragon is little different from the adults that win Grahame's approval in *The Golden Age* and *Dream Days*. The latter are, first of all, men who treat small boys as equals and live lives of scholarly or artistic leisure. Unlike most Olympians, they are imaginative and observant and willing to converse with and listen to children, enjoying their lines of thought. They are usually bachelors, but not hermits; convivial and kindly, they enjoy eating, drinking, and making merry. They also enjoy breaking with tradition in small ways—without upsetting the status quo in general. Mole and Rat in *The Wind in the Willows* are similar creatures and their relationship and conversations are not unlike those between the Boy and the Dragon.

Green speculates that all three of the main characters represent some aspect of Grahame himself: the Boy, the still vital child; the Saint, his Victorian sense of duty; the Dragon, his desires for a leisurely, scholarly, poetic, but social life-style.[28] In *The Wind in the Willows*, Grahame will also divide himself among the main characters, but he will explore more deeply the difficulties in reconciling these different projections of self.

"Bertie's Escapade"

"Bertie's Escapade," Grahame's contribution to a home newspaper, *Merry Thought*, jointly edited by his son Alastair and a friend's daughter, was not available to the public during Grahame's lifetime.[29] Written in the spring of 1907, about a year and a half before the publication of *The Wind in the Willows*, this story shows the influence of Beatrix Potter's early works. Grahame names his two rabbits Peter and Benjie and, like Potter, portrays animals, humans, and settings rather explicitly from life. Although written for children known to him, "Bertie's Escapade" is one of the more self-revealing of Grahame's works—displaying some of his adult conflicts and insecurities.

According to the story, Bertie is (as it was) the name of the pig that the Grahames kept at Mayfield, Cookham Dene. Grahame describes him as "a pig of action. 'Deeds not grunts' was his motto" (*B,* 3). One December evening, Bertie, who is moved to go carol-singing, gathers up his two rabbit pals and tries to force them to climb Chalkpit Hill (a real local landmark); Peter fortunately knows of a tunnel at the foot of the hill that leads to an elevator ("a neat little lift") manned by a mole. The lift takes them to the top of the hill and Mr. Stone's house, where they begin caterwauling and are hardly welcomed. They are chased back to the hill by dogs, reaching the mushroom that operates the elevator barely in time. Bertie, admitting his failure, attempts to make amends by inviting them all, including the mole, back to his sty for a "first-rate supper."

The enterprising pig manages to round up this supper by entering Mayfield through a window, having previously ascertained where Mr. Grahame, whom he describes as a "very careless man," keeps his keys to the pantry. He returns with two baskets full of "cold chicken, tongue, pressed beef jellies, trifle and champagne," as well as "apples, oranges, chocolate, ginger and crackers . . . gingerbeer, soda-water . . ." (*B,* 26), a menu not unlike Ratty and Mole's first lavish picnic together on the River. The would-be carolers and the mole manage to stuff themselves while proposing numerous loud toasts, "and it was three o'clock in the morning before the mole . . . made his way back to his own home, where Mrs. Mole was sitting up for him . . ." (*B,* 34).

Meanwhile, as the story goes on, the character, Mr. Grahame, is himself having a bad dream about someone raiding the pantry; this dream is followed by a vision of a City Banquet, where he first is prevented from making a speech and then gets up to reply to a toast but is dumbstruck. After "hours and hours, it seemed, in dead silence," his dream self is rudely thrown out, while the crowd sings "For he's a jolly good fellow" (*B,* 36–37).

Humorous as this dream may be in the context of the animals' partying, it is also an appropriate anxiety dream for a man whose attitude toward his city job is conflictual and one who also, after some initial literary triumphs, has been silent since his marriage some eight years before.[30] Shortly after this, of course, Grahame began to write the series of letters to his son that would grow into *The Wind in the Willows*. The immediate child audience was clearly a creative stimulus at this time.

Again, it would be a mistake to read this story or any work of Grahame's simply at the level a child would. The characters in "Bertie's Escapade," like the male friends who participate in adventures and convivial pastimes in both *The Reluctant Dragon* and *The Wind in the Willows*, belong to a special species of creature: they are, for the most part, like human grown-ups who not only enjoy the privileges of adulthood but retain and indulge the enthusiasms of boyhood—a state of being apparently desirable to Grahame, although fraught with considerable anxiety and guilt as well. *The Reluctant Dragon* manages to hold these anxieties at bay. In the character of Bertie, as in the character of Toad, boyish enthusiasm skirts delinquency and danger. In "Bertie's Escapade," Mr. Grahame's dream takes on the burden of such anxiety; *The Wind in the Willows* goes on to explore more fully the tensions inherent in trying to do as the imaginative inner child would like while living as an adult in an outer world of some natural and many societal restraints and pressures.

In contrast to the rather childlike and liberally nonconforming males that appear in many of Grahame's works of fiction, appears a line of restraining adult females. *The Headswoman* manages to deal most openly and yet both playfully and romantically with women's place in the adult world. Many of the women and girls to be met in *The Golden Age* and *Dream Days* are caricatures of such restraining powers, while the adult women in Grahame's fables are quite vicious in their maternity. Finally, *The Wind in the Willows*, which depicts a largely male society, represses, not entirely successfully, some of the anxieties Grahame evinces elsewhere about *women*'s role in generating and maintaining the restraints and pressures of adult life.

Chapter Four

Looking Backward in
The Golden Age

Shortly after its publication in the early spring of 1895, Swinburne described *The Golden Age* as "well-nigh too praiseworthy for praise."[1] Other reviewers echoed his enthusiasm. Indeed, Grahame had made a great imaginative leap in taking the prologue and five short stories published at the end of *Pagan Papers* (all of which had also appeared in the *National Observer*) and adding twelve pieces more to make a substantial collection of stories, dealing retrospectively with various incidents in the lives of five orphaned siblings and the "Olympians" in charge of them. In so doing, he found his special voice, perceptible, but not fully operative, in the personal essays.

The family unit that Grahame uses in *The Golden Age* was not new in either adult or children's novels of the nineteenth century. He distinguished himself, however, from many of his predecessors who wrote about children in large families from an adult point of view by centering the consciousness that pervades the writing in a narrator who, with generally unsentimental empathy (if some nostalgia), looks back upon himself as one of those five siblings living under the aegis of a fallible authority. Not writing for children himself, Grahame still provided a strong model for his immediate successors in children's literature, like E. Nesbit, who took the family structure and used it with some of the same empathetic but unsentimental understanding of the child's world, attaching it more firmly to the novel frame.

Except for consistency in character and in this pervasive double point of view, *The Golden Age* and its sequel, *Dream Days,* have few of the unities of the novel. Conspicuously lacking, especially when compared to nineteenth-century examples of the genre, are both development of character over time and progressive action. Conflicts are resolved within a single chapter, or not at all; neither book could be said to have a plot. The sense of order within this collection seems so minimal—or so subtle—that one can only surmise why any one story

comes after another. Yet Grahame did rearrange the stories so that
they are not in the order in which they were published periodically,
while clear exceptions to this overt lack of structure are the introduc-
tory nature of the prologue to *The Golden Age*—which delineates the
concept of the adult as Olympian—and the definite sense of an ending
that permeates the last chapters of both collections. The latter characteristic is bound up with the all-encompassing theme of childhood as
a land, like all pastoral retreats or Edens, which, once left, can rarely
be revisited.

The Prologue and First Stories

The prologue to *The Golden Age,* which expounds upon the unfair
distribution of power between the governing Olympians and "we *illuminati"* (i.e., the children) appeared in the *National Observer* as simply
"The Olympians" early in Grahame's writing career. This piece seems
to pick up its terms consciously or unconsciously from R. L. Stevenson's essay "Child's Play," where Stevenson suggests children must be
constantly bewildered by adults: "What can they think of them?
What can they make of these bearded or petticoated giants who look
down upon their games? who move upon a cloudy Olympus, following unknown designs apart from rational enjoyment?"[2]

But "The Olympians," published anonymously in September of
1891, was also firmly embedded in Grahame's own experience and
line of thought at that time. Closely preceding it in this periodical
was "The Romance of the Rail," which includes a haunting passage
about traveling to Scotland by rail (suggestive of the Grahame children's disappointing trip to live briefly with their father). Shortly,
thereafter, Grahame's "Justifiable Homicide" made its plea for the eu-
genic killing of neglectful relatives. Yet, although the thematic seeds
were there, one could not have predicted from "The Olympians" the
future flowering of these concepts into fictional characters like this
family of children and their adult enemies and friends whose personalities seem to come alive even in the fragmentary glimpses one has of
them.

The introduction to "The Olympians," which emphasizes the
plight of the orphan at the hands of insensitive and unimaginative
aunts and uncles, further confirms the personal bitterness that pervaded Grahame's writing at that time, yet evokes the image of child-

hood as fallen man's lost paradise: "Looking back to those days of old, ere the gate shut to behind me, I can see now that to children with a proper equipment of parents these things would have worn a different aspect."[3]

Of the five children who would be featured in later stories, only Harold, the youngest boy, and the narrator, who is next older male and who remains forever unnamed, appear in "The Olympians." Both boys are shown, near the end of the essay, as mischievous recipients of injustice on the part of the Olympians. This picture of the two mischievous boys is in line with the adversarial depiction of adults and children set up at the beginning of the essay, in which the Olympians are seen as effete and arbitrary—leading dreary indoor, church-going existences and never exercising the vast privileges they command for freedom in the outdoors. They busy themselves instead with petty tasks, including the supervision of the noble savages at their command: "with kindness enough as to the needs of the flesh, but after that with indifference" (*G*, 3).

The case of the children is here compared with that of Caliban, Prospero's slave on the island of Setebos in Shakespeare's *The Tempest*. This allusion, as Grahame was certainly aware, carried with it ambiguity as to the justice of the children's case. Grahame was capable of suppressing Caliban's abuses of freedom in using this allusion, just as he was capable of de-sexualizing the image of Pan. Nevertheless, unlike many of his sentimental contemporaries, but much like Stevenson, Grahame honored children not so much for their supposed innocence but for both their animal spirits and their imaginative vigor; thus the depiction of them as partaking of the savage is in no way an accident. The classical Olympians were a pretty savage lot themselves, although Grahame chose to concentrate on their present bourgeois dullness (seeing them as a "strange anaemic order of beings," *G*, 8): "On the whole, the existence of these Olympians seemed to be entirely void of interests" (*G*, 5). He emphasizes their distance from nature, particularly from the stage it provides for the imagination: "For them the orchard (a place elf-haunted, wonderful!) simply produced so many apples and cherries . . ." (*G*, 5).

The result of this double point of view is the creation of some interesting characters, both child and—more surprisingly—adult, with varying degrees of fallibility and charm. For even among the adults in this book, Grahame provides many exceptions to the Olympian rule. Appearing in this first piece, for instance, is the curate who is still capable of entering into the imaginative play of the children, willing always to give the children practical hints on how to stalk imaginary "herds of buffalo" or "to constitute himself a hostile army or a band of marauding Indians . . ." (*G,* 6).

Not until March of 1893 did the first of the *Golden Age* stories follow in the *National Observer.* In this piece, "A Whitewashed Uncle," the male Olympians emerge in full panoply of their fallibility and all of the children are introduced. The uncles in question are surveyed and found generally wanting; specifically mentioned are Uncle Thomas, who makes the children "a butt for senseless adult jokes" (*G,* 29) and Uncle George, young enough to accompany the children "cheerily around the establishment," yet falling quickly from grace when he appears to be smitten with the dubious charms of the children's governess, Miss Smedley, who is here hyperbolically described as a person of "neither accomplishments nor charms—no characteristic, in fact, but an inbred viciousness of temper and disposition" (*G,* 31).

In this story, Uncle William, "a florid, elderly man quite unmistakably nervous" (*G,* 32) newly returned from India, seems about to fail a test. A conference of four that immediately follows Uncle William's visit is about to condemn him as a beast on Selina's charge that his arrival had not even got the children a half-holiday from lessons, when Harold returns from his forced escort of Uncle William to the railway station. He is sporting four half-crowns, given him surreptitiously by this uncle. A grand reversal and white-washing of this uncle takes place. Charlotte, the youngest, murmurs, "I didn't know . . . that there were such good men anywhere in the world. I hope he'll die tonight, for then he'll go straight to heaven!" (*G,* 35). Selina is stricken at her earlier too hasty assessment. Edward suggests that they christen the piebald pig after Uncle William. That decided, the children then get down to the serious business of spending the bounty.

Prior to their publication in *Pagan Papers,* two other stories appeared together in the 20 May 1893 issue of the *National Observer.* These two, "Young Adam Cupid" and "The Finding of the Princess," emphasized another element that crops up periodically through both books of stories—attraction of young boys to the opposite sex and its romantic, almost fairy-tale associations. In the former story, the narrator and Harold are horrified to discover that their older brother, Edward, has been neglecting his rabbits because he is harboring a passion for a "nine year-old damsel" (*G,* 81), one Sabina Larkin, daughter of the neighboring farmer with whom the boys are always having border skirmishes. Dragged shortly thereafter, along with his Aunt Eliza, on enforced Sunday visits of state to local farmers and cottagers, the narrator is pleased to see that Sabina is herself put off Edward by Aunt Eliza's story of Edward's recent meanness to Charlotte. Sabina, at the next opportunity, sticks out her tongue at Edward, flouncing past him and causing him to run home to torment the chickens and smoke "a half-consumed cigar he had picked up on the road" (*G,* 88). The narrator concludes that the crisis has passed as regards his brother, but then, so fatal are women, is himself suddenly and ironically smitten with Sabina.

"The Finding of the Princess" shows the narrator skipping his geography lesson as he is wont to do. Unable to persuade Harold to accompany him, the narrator first dabbles awhile in the well and then heads for the woods, following a stream and playing an elaborate game of pirates in Tom Sawyer fashion, until he comes upon some wire-netting and a hedge that bar his way. Scrambling through a small passage made by a rabbit, he suddenly finds himself in a magnificently cultivated garden replete with goldfish and peacocks. In keeping with his recent passage through a huge hedge, the garden takes on for him the quality of the grounds of Sleeping Beauty's castle and, exploring, he is not at all surprised eventually to come upon a woman and a man engaged in playful conversation while she attempts to disengage her hand from his. He immediately identifies them in his own mind with the newly aroused Princess and her Prince. When they notice him and the man asks where he has come from, the boy explains that he "came up the stream" and "was only looking for a Princess." The following conversation (with its sly allusion to Charles Kingsley's *The Water Babies* [1863]) then ensues:

"Then you are a water-baby," he replied. "And what do you think of the Princess, now you've found her?"
"I think she is lovely," I said. . . . "But she's wide-awake, so I suppose somebody has kissed her!" (*G,* 60–61)

The man is amused, the Princess, embarrassed; the boy is invited to lunch. The boy accepts the attentions of the grown-ups as his due, eats heartily, thinks the elegantly dressed footman is a Lord, and after lunch accepts two half-crowns and a suggestion from the man to go look at the gold fish—receiving from the Princess a farewell kiss. The narrator depicts these scenes in ways that emphasize the self-centered naiveté of his boy-self, so much so that some modern readers insist that in this story the Olympian point of view is in the forefront: the boy-self is patronized and made the butt of the man-self's jokes.[4]

The story ends with the boy falling asleep in the garden and awaking alone in a "wild, unreasoning panic" (G, 64). He rushes home, is discovered entering by the scullery window, and sent to bed tealess. However, the reader soon learns that, as usual, the lower orders are countermanding the orders of the chief Olympians: a "sympathetic housemaid" feeds the boy, who thus falls asleep, replete, to dream of a "rose-flushed Princess" (G, 64).

The fear of punishment rarely deters Grahame's children from engaging in behavior that will bring it down upon them but they, as in this case, are often saved from the worst effects of punishment. Yet, there is, as at the end of this story, frequently a psychic cloud that gathers about the end of like adventures, especially when they are solitary to the narrator—a recognition that exercise of the imagination holds its terrors as well as its joys.

"Burglars," first published in the *National Observer* in June of 1893, shows two adults similarly engaged in romantic activities. Unlike "The Finding of the Princess," this story depicts the three boys in control of the situation, perhaps because the lady in question is their Aunt Mary—not likely to evoke romantic longings in their own young breasts. Her suitor is an affected young curate (carefully distinguished from the imaginative curate of the prologue). Here the two older boys (in order to confirm Edward's contention that the two are "spooning") rouse Harold to slide down the drainpipe and spy on Aunt Mary and her beau as they stroll in the moonlight.

Harold is caught spying by the curate and not only puts up a fake howl, but claims that he had seen what looked like burglars in the garden before the couple's arrival and had come down to reconnoiter. This tale is given credence not by Harold's lurid details, culled from a recent "Penny Dreadful," but by the other two boys' coming to the rescue, providing larcenous sound effects in the background. In the ensuing confusion, Harold escapes to be comforted by the cook, and the curate has the opportunity to demonstrate a statement made earlier at table that he "feared no foe" (G, 93). Aunt Maria cries, "O Mr. Hodgetts! . . . you are brave! for my sake do not be rash!" (G,

103). And, the narrator notes, "He was not rash." Nevertheless, the curate gets the credit for frightening away the burglars, while the narrator gets the last word in a manner perhaps too subtle to be credibly childlike: shortly thereafter, hearing the curate joke over afternoon tea about "the moral courage required for taking the last piece of bread and butter" (*G,* 104), the narrator mutters Aunt Maria's plea just loudly enough for the curate to hear and, triumphant, quickly makes his escape.

The last of the early *Golden Age* stories to appear in *Pagan Papers,* "Snowbound," was published in the *National Observer* in September 1893, just a month before the publication of *Pagan Papers.* It shows the children weary and irritable after seeing the Twelfth Night mummers the previous evening. They are "housebound" and trying to occupy themselves. Selina is off on some unnamed occupation, but the other four are gathered in one room where Edward is imitating the mummers, and Harold, who thus became known and endeared to the reading public for his invention of strangely prosaic imaginative characters, is playing "clubmen," a solitary game that involves "a measured progress round the room arm-in-arm with an imaginary companion of reverend years, with occasional halts at imaginary clubs . . ." (*G,* 122–23). Charlotte and the narrator are both in the window seat, gazing out at the snow, a pastime which seems to increase Charlotte's dejection at having been told, by Miss Smedley at the breakfast table, that fairies did not exist.

The narrator attempts to cheer Charlotte by reading to her from King Arthur, but unluckily opens the volume to the tragic tale of Balin and Balan, causing her to cry. Edward comes to the rescue with "a jolly story" of unrequited love between a duck and stork, which, of course, fails to console Charlotte. The narrator claims that such was Edward's "stupid inability to see the real point in anything" (*G,* 127). This characterization of Edward as an insensitive blusterer is enhanced by his refusal to notice Charlotte's reaction and his immediate recruitment of Harold to play a dragon to his "King Gearge," of Charlotte to be the princess, and of the reluctant narrator to be the doctor. The morning ends in a brawl between Edward and the others that is described as "mixed, chaotic and Arthurian," until the lunch bell, acting not unlike the "Holy Grail itself," stills "a riot of warring passions." (*G,* 129).

The ways in which the children are introduced in these initial stories, through dialogue and action, are typical of all the stories that follow. They are never described physically and their ages are mentioned only when essential to the action. Yet the salient characteristics of the individual children are set by these early stories: Edward remains the domineering blusterer; Selina is outspoken; the narrator often wanders off alone but is generally sensitive to the needs of the two younger children; Charlotte cries easily and is given to verbal faux pas; Harold is both an escape artist and a master at occupying himself in intriguing ways.

Certain stylistic characteristics seem to be constant throughout the stories as well. The adult audience is implicit in that the style of exposition and description is close to that of the *Pagan Papers* essays: still rather archaic in diction and heavy with literary allusion. But dialogue assumes a much larger place than in the essays and the children tell each other interesting digressive stories as Edward does in "Burglars" where he defines "spooning" by telling the story of his friend Bobby Ferris—who earned pocket money acting as a liaison between his sister and her suitor and attempted to keep the romance and his income going after both had dried up, by himself writing notes between the two. Another stylistic aspect of these stories is the play on settings of various kinds, making them take on special atmosphere through allusion, as with the hedged garden in "The Lost Princess."

Grahame goes on to create other interesting episodes in the lives of these children, but most of the major themes or motifs that will be explored in both *The Golden Age* and *Dream Days* are also already anticipated in these early stories. These can be broadly categorized as (1) relationships between adults and children, (2) sibling relationships, (3) children's imaginative play, (4) young boys' romantic interest in the opposite sex, and (5) the transient nature of childhood.

Olympians versus Illuminati

As is already apparent, grown-ups and particularly imaginative adult males and affectionate females of the lower classes do not come off altogether badly in these stories. On the one hand, a special group of scorned grown-ups, like Aunt Eliza, Farmer Larkin, and Miss Smedley, provoke mischievous rebellion through their dominating and seemingly capricious enforcement of Olympian codes of conduct; some, like the young and "rash" curate and the two uncles, make themselves ridiculous in the eyes of the children. On the other hand, materially indulgent adults—like Uncle Willie, the Princess's suitor, and the sympathetic housemaid—or imaginative grown-ups, like the curate, win the hearts and minds of the children. Further interesting to see, in the course of *The Golden Age,* is how certain adults who seem at first irrevocably committed to the Olympian side of the battlefield are able to surprise the children with sudden generosity and understanding.

"A Harvesting" is one of the pieces in which the narrator ventures out alone, escaping not from adults at this time, but from Edward's bullying. The boy heads for the village, imagining himself to be a kind of Mungo Park, the African explorer. On the way he has a rude awakening, bumping into an elderly clergyman who is also daydreaming. The latter apologizes to the boy profusely; they take to each other as fellow dreamers, and, in a courtly manner, the clergyman invites the narrator to enter the nearby gate to his home, offering him "some poor refreshment" (*G,* 111).

The narrator recognizes this gentleman as the Rector famed in the village for scholarship and as the author of "a real book" (*G,* 112). He is led into the Rector's study containing a piano on which he is invited to strum to his heart's content, an unusual boon, while the Rector immediately loses himself in his books—interrupting their absorption only by asking a rhetorical question about German scholarship to which the narrator replies according to his limited but confident understanding of the subject. This conversation, seemingly satisfying to them both, continues swimmingly until the Rector's housekeeper interrupts, bullying him to have his tea in the garden—an interruption to which the narrator hardly himself objects.

The final scene depicts a snarling tramp approaching the Rector, who had in his usual manner already distributed all of his loose change to earlier supplicants. The tramp abuses the Rector for his refusal, but shortly thereafter is seen assisting his frowsy female companion to carry her burdens, in "a dim approach to tenderness" (*G,* 117). The Rector draws a charitable moral from this scene, that "love lives and shines out in the unlikeliest places," although "one must stoop" to see it (*G,* 118). With this timely moral echoing in his head, the narrator trots home without his usual awakening dread of Olympian punishment.[5]

The kindly, scholarly, otherworldly Rector is the exemplar of the childlike man admired by Grahame. His life-style is also probably close to Grahame's choice. In particular, the Rector's study appears to be "the ideal I dreamed but failed to find. None of your feminine fripperies here! . . . This man, it was seen, groaned under no aunts" (*G*, 112). This room, free of female influence, is untidily full of books and "a faint aroma of tobacco" (*G*, 112), all of which signal a singular freedom to the narrator as boy and possibly to Grahame as man as well. The Rector's talking to the boy as an equal is characteristic also of all the admired adults in Grahame's writing. This standard of gentlemanly behavior is unknown among relatives.

"The Argonauts" features Grahame's rare portrait of a grown female who has these attractive attributes. She, however, as is clear from the context, is considered mad by her society, and her female keeper is more threatening than the Rector's housekeeper. The three boys meet this "Medea" on the occasion when Edward has persuaded them to commandeer Farmer Larkin's boat in order to play the game of Jason and the Argonauts (which Harold has started in the pig trough) with some real style. Selina is left behind because she might get puritanical about the theft and Charlotte in case she might fall out of the boat in a daydream.

Landing in new territory, another garden which seems to have something magical about it, and exploring a sundial that says, fittingly, "TIME: TRYETH: TROUTH," Harold and the narrator (Edward has disappeared) are greeted by a figure, "dark-haired, supple," who rushes to the rescue when Harold falls off the sundial and skins his knee (*G*, 150). When he recovers she asks them immediately to play games with her, claiming that she has been shut up for one hundred and fifty years. She plays "hide and seek" with a gusto that belies this age and also the mythical allusion to Medea. Her fervor reminds the narrator of Persephone's joy on her return to earth. This allusion to the myth of Persephone turns out to be a curiously inverted one: when asked the meaning of the words on the sundial she depicts herself as having been imprisoned in this place to forget a lover (not as being captured by a lover and asked to forget her mother, Ceres). Her sad lot is confirmed by the approach of an elderly forbidding woman who says, "Lucy," sharply "in a tone with *aunt* writ large over it" (*G*, 154). This presumptive aunt chases the boys away to the shore where they reunite with Edward and set sail for home to plague Farmer Larkin once more.

Special shades of the Olympian versus child relationship are brought into play here. A number of the adults attractive to the children seem also to have their own Olympians to contend with, although if they are male and bachelors like the Rector, they need conform only when they feel like it. The role of tyrannous female keeper is, however, epitomized by a duenna, Lucy's aunt.

Another type of favored adult also emerges in "The Roman Road"—the artist. This occupation was obviously appealing to the aesthetic audience of the Yellow Book in which the story first appeared. Starting off down a road called by the children "The Knights' Road," the narrator, leaving behind an uncomfortable home situation, builds a daydream upon the expression "all roads lead to Rome," and imagines a dream city made up of bits and pieces of municipal architecture familiar to him locally. "Down a delectable street of cloud-built palaces, I was mentally pacing, when I happened upon the Artist" (*G*, 165). The boy knows enough not actually to interrupt this "*genus irritabile*" but sets himself down for a good long stare interrupted first by the artist's absentmindedly offering him his tobacco pouch and then by the artist's courteous greeting and inquiry as to how far he is going. The boy replies, "I *was* thinking of going on to Rome: but I've put it off" (*G*, 166). This leads to the discovery that the artist, miraculously, lives in Rome, "in a sort of shanty" about half the year.

On further persistent inquiry, the boy discovers more about the artist, including the fact that he has also traveled to most places in the world except "the Fortunate Islands" (*G*, 168). The boy likes this man for both his openness and his seriousness and so asks the man a confidential question, "Wouldn't you like . . . to find a city without any people in it at all?" The dream city the narrator then describes is full of well-furnished shops and houses freely open to the dreamer. Further details include inviting friends and no "relations at all unless they promised they'd be pleasant" (*G*, 170).

While pointing out that Marcus Aurelius, the Stoic, would not have approved of this city, the artist too gets into the swing of things and starts imagining who might join them there. After the narrator explains that Lancelot and Robinson Crusoe and "all the nice men in the stories who don't marry the Princess" will have preceded them, the artist offers "the men who have never come off . . . who try like the rest, but get knocked out, or somehow miss—or break down or get bowled over in the melee. . . . (*G*, 172–73). This is a statement that the narrator admits he did not quite understand at the time, yet the boy and the man find themselves in perfect general accord and make a pact to meet and stay together in this dream city.

Meanwhile, the narrator has to return "downheartedly" to "the house where I never could do anything right" (*G*, 174). On the way, he consoles himself with another daydream of arriving in this dream city in time to see the entrance of his new friend, whom he imagines as a kind of knight, encountered as he was on this "Knights' Road," who will arrive in shining armor (*G*, 175).

The capacity for entering into such paradisial daydreams is apparently the quality of the artist and the essense of the contrast between him and the rest—"uncles, vicars and other grown-up men"—who consider such dreams "tomfoolery" (*G*, 174–75). Giving us further insight into the characteristics and values that distinguish good Olympians from bad, this story has a level for adult readers that, unlike "The Finding of the Princess," does not ask them to participate in making fun of the naiveté of the young. What goes over the head of the narrator's boy-self is the frustration of the artist entailed in his never having reached "the Fortunate Islands" and his references to the stoicism of Marcus Aurelius in his acceptance of worldly defeat. Yet the boy's image of the man as a knight in shining armor has a double-edged irony: it contradicts the probable "worldly" truth but may be a perception of a finer, inner truth about the unsuccessful adult.

The semienchanted gardens of "The Lost Princess" and "The Argonauts" seem connected with a romantic view of women, while the dream city in this story and the perfect room in "A Harvesting" are recurring images of felicitous space in Grahame's work—places that often *exclude* women. They are complexly connected here and elsewhere with the Edenic pastoral, and, to some extent, with apocalyptical imagery in the embodiment of the theme of the transcience of childhood.

"Exit Tyrannus" proves that even notoriously oppressive Olympians do not always stay in their assigned roles. The children's condemnation of Miss Smedley, the governess, is always clearly hyperbolic, but this story does much to redeem her image and to suggest the finally rather benign and forgiving picture of Olympians that is filtered through this double point of view. Unbeknown as yet to the children, the departure of Miss Smedley will be one of the first markers of the end of childhood. At first this event is anticipated with considerable glee as a time "at least free from one familiar scourge" (*G*, 193). The children plan a grand celebration. Yet, when the day actually arrives Miss Smedley takes the children by surprise at breakfast where they feel strangely aggrieved by her starting to cry.

The balance of power between the Olympians and the illuminati is further disturbed because there are no lessons that morning and the very lack of their usual grievances becomes a grievance to the children. Looking back, the narrator attributes his "growing feeling of depression" on that day to "the innate conservatism of youth" which "asks neither poverty nor riches but only immunity from change" (*G,* 197). None of the children can summon up the spirit to proceed with the planned festivities, and the three boys find themselves reminiscing about the good things Miss Smedley had done for them in the past that they had forgotten, although neither Edward nor the narrator will openly attribute their gloom to her departure.

"Exit Tyrannus" gives hint of an emotional impediment in children, in part attributable to the Olympians themselves, but also partly a matter of the children's natural self-centeredness, which prevents them from perceiving and empathizing with the needs and emotions of adults and often of each other. The early strictures on emotional display placed on young boys in particular are emphasized in the ending of this story when Edward, for instance, has to participate in the violent activity of chopping wood in order to deal with his emotions. Grahame does not suggest that things should be otherwise; recognition that children are often unfair, unsympathetic, and even cruel toward adults and others, although capable of being outwardly generous and inwardly moved upon occasion, is part of Grahame's unsentimentalized view of childhood. He shared this recognition with R. L. Stevenson, who, in his essay "Child's Play," describes children as displaying at times "an arrogance of disregard that is truly staggering."[6] Richard Jefferies's portrayal of his hero, young Bevis, in *Wood Magic,* perpetrates no illusions about children's treatment of animals and, in this regard as well, Grahame shows little sentimentality about children's activities and reactions—the cat always runs when they appear. If the Olympians are hardly godlike, the *illuminati* are, in many ways, unenlightened.

The Siblings

The ages of the five children are never made entirely clear in the course of the two books. All seem to be under twelve. Edward is the oldest male and Harold the youngest. Selina is the older female and Charlotte, the younger. In terms of inheriting toys, Charlotte is clearly the baby of the family. The narrator is somewhere in-between

the two pairs, but the sequence is murky. Is Edward or Selina the
oldest sibling? Is Selina actually older than the narrator? The narrator
often allies himself with the two younger children; but later when
Edward goes off to school in "Lusisti Satis," the narrator claims to be
next in command in a hierarchy that is, however, probably based on
sex rather than age.

Such a sexual hierarchy would reflect Victorian custom and is suggested by the steady stream of invective on Edward's part against the
weakness and general uselessness of females and also by the occasions,
as in "The Argonauts" and "Burglars," when the three boys are together and the girls excluded. Nevertheless, Selina and Harold are
frequent companions, while the narrator feels a special affinity with
Charlotte. In imaginative play in particular, sex lines are crossed. The
role of Tristram, for instance, is always reserved for Charlotte in acting out Arthurian material. Although the children generally form a
solid front before the Olympians, "Snowbound" depicts the tension
among the ranks, and two of the other stories, "What They Talked
About" and "A Falling Out," deal centrally with other aspects of the
sibling relationship.

The focus is on Selina in "What They Talked About" and on her
role as "eldest lady." First she is seen "toying, in her affected feminine way" (G, 134), with some cork in the ginger beer to which Edward is treating the others after having received the customary
monetary reward for a session in the dentist's chair. Selina falls from
grace quickly when she takes "a most unfairly long pull" (G, 135) on
the third bottle and announces that she is going for a walk. The other
children, led by Edward, try to figure out what Selina, who is next
seen walking with "those Vicarage girls," could possibly be talking
about. Edward asserts that girls have nothing possibly of interest to
discuss for "They don't *know* anything; they can't *do* anything . . .
and they don't care about anything . . ." (G, 137). The others also
have no idea and Charlotte cannot enlighten them for she too has been
excluded as being too little.

Selina's possible allegiance with the Olympians is intimated by the
narrator's musing aloud about similarly confusing Olympian talk that
he has overheard. Harold, watching a rabbit whom they have invited
to the festivities, notes that rabbits seem to converse in much the
same way as Selina and her friends do, eliciting from Edward the final
statement that "I'll bet they don't talk such rot as those girls do!"
(G, 139).

Selina is shown in a more sympathetic light in "A Falling Out," where she is unjustly attacked both verbally and physically by a distraught Harold when she comes to hear his multiplication tables and thus rescue him from *durance vile* in the school room after hours. An immediately remorseful Harold is determined to find "some atonement heroic enough to salve the wrong" (*G*, 226). He decides to buy Selina a dolls' tea set that she has been coveting for months. The narrator and he go into a huddle to scrape together the money by various means—break-ins to savings, loans, and extortion of debts—and Harold schemes to present the tea set at a party that Selina is planning at five the next day. In order to make the gift as ostentatious as possible, he continues to alienate himself from Selina, who, therefore, "moped for the rest of the evening . . ." (*G*, 229).

After an anxious trip to town, Harold finds the teaset just where it has been for the last six months, buys it, and has it wrapped and held at the shop while he windowshops and explores the town, becoming so absorbed that he loses track of time and races for home—only to discover halfway that he has left the tea things behind. Sobbing hysterically, Harold turns back, almost running under a dog cart driven by Farmer Larkin. In spite of the fact that Harold has recently been abusing his ducks, the farmer turns out to be surprisingly sympathetic; he drives Harold back to town to pick up the teaset and on the way home commiserates about the multiplication tables.

All is made up, of course, by Harold's gesture. Thus Selina is redeemed by this story, although she often appears elsewhere as the one who might well develop into an insensitive and unimaginative "aunt," for, as the narrator notes in "The Argonauts" (the story that follows "What They Talked About"), she had "just reached that disagreeable age when one begins to develop a conscience" (*G*, 147), and her interest in the Vicarage girls is certainly a bad sign. The emergence of Farmer Larkin as a fairly sympathetic character is significant here, too, and the narrator, when he hears from Harold about their meeting, admits "really, when I heard the story, it began to dawn upon me that those Olympians must have certain good points, far down in them, and that I should have to leave off abusing them someday" (*G*, 234). Like the redemption of Miss Smedley, Farmer Larkin's redemption contributes to the sense of an ending in *The Golden Age*.

Although the narrator notes in "What They Talked About" that "it was the custom of our Family to meet with physical coercion any independence of action in individuals" (*G*, 136), the separating force that age and change will have on the children as siblings is nowhere more clearly shown than in the end story, "Lusisti Satis" (enough play), when the ranks are broken abruptly by Edward's departure for boarding school; yet, Edward, too, not so much by age as by personality, is often shown earlier, like Selina, as separate from the other children, and his future development as a rampaging and familially iconoclastic schoolboy should come as no surprise to any of the readers.

Some biographical speculation with regard to the personalities of these siblings is not entirely out of line. The fictional family created by Grahame is both like his own and different from it in certain important ways. Grahame's own family was, of course, under Granny Ingles, in virtually the same orphaned plight. Grahame was also the child vaguely in the middle of four (rather than five) siblings; Edward might well have been based to some extent on his older brother Willie, Selina on his older sister Helen, and Harold on his younger brother Roland. No one corresponded to Charlotte in Grahame's real family. Her presence and special quality of tenderness found in the narrator's relation to her reminds us to look not only to Grahame's own sublimated needs for intimacy in his childhood and later bachelorhood, but also calls to mind the hallowed nature of sibling relationships—especially between brother and sister—that is a pervasive element in Victorian life and literature, often exalted over nonfamilial, marital intimacy. The antics of the five children somewhat mask this pairing off into intimate couples, but it provides an additional nuance to the familial scene.

Moreover, in terms of understanding the ways in which personal experience turns into fiction, one might well think not only of the narrator but possibly also of both Edward and Harold as partaking of the complex nature of Kenneth Grahame himself. The narrator's sensitivity and liking for solitude, Harold's imaginative fervor and originality, Edward's physical heartiness, domineering ways, and schoolboy antics, could all have belonged to Grahame himself at various stages of his boyhood. Once considered in that light, Edward's characteristics seem the least likely to have belonged to Grahame himself, yet neither did Edward have to be modeled on Grahame's older brother, for previous literature for both adults and children had provided many examples of such young boys—Tom Tulliver in *The Mill on the Floss* was certainly such a one and, in children's literature,

Robinson Jefferies's adolescent Bevis, Mark Twain's Tom Sawyer, and Thomas Hughes's Tom Brown, of *Tom Brown's School Days* (1857). Following Grahame are Rudyard Kipling's schoolboy heroes in *Stalky and Company* (1899) and E. Nesbit's Oswald of the Bastable family novels—all of much the same mischievous yet sympathetically viewed ilk.[7]

Imaginative Play

Two different types of imaginative play emerge in the stories of *The Golden Age* and *Dream Days*. Grahame frequently depicts the kind of imaginative play that Stevenson describes in his "Child's Play": an acting out of stories requiring "lay figures and stage properties." Stevenson writes, "When the story comes to fighting, [the child] must rise, get something in the way of a sword and have a set-to with a piece of furniture until he's out of breath."[8] The depiction in "The Argonauts" of Harold playing Jason in the pig trough belongs to this highly active type of imaginative play; this same story begins with a discussion of the ways in which these children have only recently come to know and like classical heroes, giving them the seal of approval by acting out their mythic activities, which do not displace, however, the antics of fairy-tale heroes.

Grahame, unlike Stevenson, seems to assume also less explicit, usually solitary exercise of the imagination on the part of children, a kind of daydreaming or castle building, often connected with nature or evocative places or objects; Stevenson rather emphatically denies that children have this capacity for original fantasizing. Of particular interest for its depiction of both capacities in children is a relatively late story, "A Holiday," which first appeared in the *New Review* in March 1895, in the same issue as "Lusisti Satis." Significantly, Grahame placed "A Holiday" right after the prologue in *The Golden Age,* thus setting a particular tone and emphasis for the book as a whole quite different from that set by "A Whitewashed Uncle," which first appeared in this second place among the stories in *Pagan Papers.*

Initially, "A Holiday" is pervaded with a sense of a beginning. The story opens on a glorious early spring morning; it is someone's birthday and therefore a whole holiday from lessons. Here traditional elements of rebirth and liberation set off the tone of joy in the narrator's voice as he describes his boy self running "through the meadows, frisking happy heels in the face of Nature laughing responsive." He is joined by Charlotte and the two enjoy this "brimming sun-bathed world" silently, for "the glow and glory of existing in this perfect morning were satisfaction full and sufficient" (G, 14).

After this silent communion, the narrator inquires about both Harold and Edward. The former, it seems, is engrossed in a solitary, self-initiated game of "muffin-man"—his latest craze and one rather incomprehensible to the others, although as the narrator (always sympathetic to creation of imaginary settings) points out, "to pass along busy streets of your own building, forever ringing an imaginary bell and offering airy muffins of your own make to a bustling thronging crowd of your own creation" (G, 15) has certain esoteric joys. Meanwhile Edward, Charlotte admits, is approaching them from the rear, planning a surprise attack in the guise of a grizzly bear.

After elaborate active imaginative play, the narrator slips away on his own for "the passion and call of the divine morning were high in [his] blood" (G, 19). He responds to this call of the wild by dancing and singing, intoxicated by the air which "was wine, the moist earth-smell wine, the lark's song, the wafts from the cow shed at top of the field, the pant and smoke of a distant train—all were wine—or song was it? or odour, this unity they all blent into" (G, 19–20).

Eventually, a personified wind seems to speak to him—enticing him to go off together "arm in arm"; the narrator finds the wind a "whimsical comrade," leading him first to "a pair of lovers, silent, face to face o'er a discreet unwinking stile" (G, 21), a scene that seems to harmonize with the landscape as it has never done before, and then he sees "the peerless bad boy of the village" (G, 23) sneaking into the vestry window to steal the Vicar's biscuits, an act for which the narrator feels, like the amoral wind, no condemnation; he sees a hawk drop down to catch its prey, and finds a dead hedgehog for which Nature seems to shed no tear. He finally is brought short at the village whipping post, which reminds him of worldly law and order and returns him to the hard world of the Olympians.

The holiday that began so auspiciously ends ominously. At home again the narrator finds "the moral of the whipping post . . . working itself out." Charlotte, deserted by Edward, is weeping; Harold has fallen into the duck pond and been sent off to bed; the narrator himself is "seized upon and accused of doing something [he] had never thought of. And [his] frame of mind was such, that [he] could only wish most heartily [he] had done it" (G, 26). Even the imaginative play of the children holds in itself a threat of discord and a dread of the future, just as even the most pagan and amoral vision of the natural world cannot avoid confronting death, while the civilized world has invented severe punishments for intoxicated abandonment to joy.

The particular nature of the narrator's fantasizing play with the wind deserves further examination. The notion of the companionship of the wind and its force for inspiration has a long history stemming from myth, but two of Grahame's immediate predecessors in children's literature had used the personification of the wind as a kind of maternal protector and guide in the education of young boys. In George MacDonald's *At the Back of the North Wind* (1871) and Richard Jefferies's *Wood Magic* (1881), the personified wind brings a vision of comfort in either this world or the next. Grahame's creation of the wind as a masculine, amoral companion "the trickster, the hypocrite" (*G, 21*) is an interesting development of the topos. Although later, in the Man in the Moon of the last *Dream Days* story, and in the Great God Pan of *The Wind in the Willows,* Grahame was to project a comforting paternal vision of nature, here, in contrast to either MacDonald's or Jefferies's diverse yet evident faiths, Grahame cannot sustain a sense of rebirth and hope, even among children. One is reminded that, in his *Pagan Papers* essays, communion with nature usually ended with a visit to the pub—an escape available only to Olympians.

"Alarums and Excursions" and "The Blue Room" are other stories that deal largely with the more active, derivative, and communal types of imaginative play in children. In "Alarums and Excursions," the narrator and Harold interrupt a game of Knights of the Round Table, with Charlotte as Tristram, in order to follow a real troup of cavalry whom the narrator claims are off to battle with the French. Eventually they find themselves in unfamiliar territory with the riders nowhere in sight, and the narrator feeling a sense of heavy responsibility placed on him by Harold's perfect faith in his judgment. Fortunately, they are met by the doctor in his carriage and he drives them home. The doctor turns out to be one of those adults who can join in child's play, and he answers their inquiries about "the coming battle"—which he claims has been "put off, on account of the change in the weather"—in a satisfactory way, regaling them with "blood-curdling narratives of personal adventure in tented fields" (*G, 49*).

In "The Blue Room," in contrast, the children's imaginative play confounds another Olympian of the ridiculous sort—a newly arrived

tutor with antiquarian interests who, on this first night, is put to
sleep in the Blue Room, which serves the children as a back passage
for clandestine night raids on the kitchen. On this occasion, the children, wakened by a rattling storm, decide to go down for biscuits.
As they creep through the Blue Room they are inspired to act out a
silent scene in a moonlit patch "in which Selina was stabbed slowly
and with unction, and her corpse borne from the chamber by the
ruthless cavalier" (*G*, 214). The fact that there has been an audience
for their "dumbest of dumb shows" is revealed not only by the hasty
departure of the tutor the next day, but by the subsequent appearance
in *Psyche: A Journal of the Unseen* (to which Uncle Thomas subscribes)
an anonymous description of their house and of the ghostly reenacted
murder.

"The Secret Drawer" returns to the solitary musing. The narrator
is commandeered to escort Uncle Thomas while he is "pottering
about the house." On this tour they land in an unused room that
must once have served as a kind of feminine boudoir, in which stands
an old bureau that Uncle Thomas admires in his dilettantish way. He
comments also that it must have a secret drawer and rushes off to
smoke, leaving the boy behind, "still vibrating to those magic sylla-
bles 'secret drawer' " (*G*, 182). The boy suddenly feels that all hope
of rescue from financial straits lies within this "magic drawer" (*G*,
184).

As the narrator approaches the bureau the room seems to him "possessed . . . by a sort of hush of expectation" (*G*, 184). He immediately finds a button hook and some foreign stamps, but no drawer;
after a period of despair, he returns for one last try. He finds the
drawer filled not with a pirate's but "a real boy's hoard" (*G*, 188).
This trove is at first a disappointment but then it forms a link and
special tie between the narrator and a boy of the past. He returns the
drawer, still filled with gilt buttons, birds' eggs, and the like, to its
place, for the next boy to find. He must pause a moment to get his
bearings before returning to his siblings who are playing a noisy game
of bears or bandits, so displaced in space and time does he feel. This
perception of the possibility of generations of children being linked
with one another by their tastes and desires is one of the few intimations of immutability that *The Golden Age* affords.

An aspect of interest here is the combination of practical need with
the romantic quest for hidden treasure. Over and over, children's literature both before and after Grahame recognizes that children, while

especially taken by romantic schemes for obtaining wealth, participate
in adult anxieties about ways and means. They very early engage not
only in primitive bartering systems but in relatively complicated accounting systems involving the coin of the realm. In "A Falling
Out," Grahame actually produces a parodic accounting sheet for Harold's acquisition of the necessary cash to purchase the dolls' tea set for
Selina; "The Secret Drawer" depicts the complex system of loans
among the children and with the servants, who are far more generous
than relatives. Grahame's own sense of his relatives' lack of generosity
even up to the time of composition of these works may play a part in
this emphasis on short rations and large needs.[9]

Here, as elsewhere in these stories, one finds it hard to sort and
categorize the mix of the adult and childlike, especially in those passages where the imaginative faculty is largely solitary and played out
not dramatically but in the narrator's mind. Grahame seems to have
been a man who valued and kept in touch with much that was childlike in his own personality. However, as many in examining these
stories might note, the narrator's account of the feelings of his boy
self does not always seem appropriate to the preadolescent.[10] Nevertheless, Grahame's general demonstration of the wide potentiality of
the imaginative faculty in the child—not limited to acting out
alone—gives a believable depth to the characterization of the narrator
and may indeed reflect the reality of the unusual, but by no means
unique, child.

Sexual Attraction and Romance

A number of the stories in *Dream Days* center on a young boy's
attraction to the opposite sex, treated as a somewhat ludicrous but
inevitable impediment to true boyhood (as in "Young Adam Cupid"),
or as a romantic aspect of the imaginative faculty (as in "The Finding
of the Princess"). In *The Golden Age,* however, only one other story
picks up the theme of attraction to the opposite sex, endowing it
with an oblique sexuality to which certain of Grahame's first readers
objected.[11] This was "Sawdust and Sin," in which the narrator eaves-
drops on a session of Charlotte's with her dolls, after she has unwit-
tingly interrupted his own imaginative tropical adventure in the belt
of rhododendrums along the side of the pond.

Charlotte has set up two of her dolls to listen to a bedtime story,
a somewhat conflated version of *Alice's Adventures in Wonderland:* Jerry,

from Japan, who "has a latent deviltry in his slant eyes," and Rosa—
demurely and typically British—"from her flaxen poll to the stout
calves she displayed so liberally" (*G,* 69). Charlotte's storytelling
forms a counterpoint to Jerry's sexual maneuvers, for the narrator
imagines Jerry, who finds it difficult to sit upright, as gradually man-
aging to lay his head on Rose's shoulder and putting his arm around
her—causing her to fall over in a dead faint, to be righted by Charlotte—only to have Jerry, "overmastered by his passion," fall across
her lap. In spite of Rosa's subsequent "full-bodied surrender" (*G,*
73), Jerry is immediately punished by Charlotte, who spanks him,
and not much later he is carried off by the family dog, whom the
narrator envisions as a messenger from Hell, to be seen no more.

Charlotte treats her dolls maternally, seeing Jerry as nothing but a
naughty child, but the narrator's imagination is not particularly familial or even romantic. His is erotic; when Rosa falls over, "her
limbs . . . rigid, her eyes glassy," the narrator asks suggestively,
"What had Jerry been doing? It must have been something very bad
. . ." (*G,* 72). The degree of the narrator's sympathy with Jerry—in
spite of the clear racial as well as sexual innuendos in this fantasy—
makes it worthwhile considering in the light of Grahame's general attitude toward women, expressed elsewhere. This story seems to pick
up both Grahame's tendency to depict women as maternal oppressors
and as temptresses. Here even charming Charlotte takes on the Olympian aspect of arbitrary maternal authority, while Rosa is clearly no
innocent: "in character she was of the blameless order of those who
have not yet been found out" (*G,* 69). The prudish objections of Grahame's contemporaries in relation to this story were perhaps mis-
placed. Moreover, children are certainly capable of sexual fantasies;
yet here, as in "The Secret Drawer," the experience of the narrator as
man, not boy, seems to govern the particular details of the fantasy.

An End to Games

Both the title of this group of stories and its prologue imply a
sense of an ending. The title, *The Golden Age,* is an allusion to wonderful times of a mythical past that will never come again; the prologue begins with the notion of the gates of a biblical paradise closing
behind the child and ends with a nostalgic allusion to the romance
paradise of Arcadia which the narrator once inhabited. Through reference, incident, imagery, and setting, as well as eventual placement of

stories, the inevitability of change and the impossibility of return to childhood are concepts that pervade *The Golden Age,* but, as might be expected, nowhere as thoroughly as in the last story, "Lusisti Satis."

Here the Olympians try in vain to keep from the children the fact that Uncle Thomas, who is used frequently as a messenger from their household to the outside world, has been commissioned to find out about (boarding) schools, a subject that the children have always recognized as constituting an "inevitable bourne" (words used usually to describe death rather than departure for school) (*G,* 241). With it now looming over them as "a grim spectre" (again the death image), they inquire where they can about what school is like and get contradictory reports from contemporaries.

Edward, when he learns that it is to be he alone who is sent, hovers and alternates between keen anticipation and dread, obviously enjoying some of the attention and preparation. Meanwhile, with similar ambivalence, the narrator anticipates his new role in the house, as elder boy, leader, and thus liaison between the Olympians and the children. When the dread day arrives, the other children accompany Edward in his new hard bowler hat (from which he seems to derive some consolation) to the railroad station, where he departs with his usual bravado. Left behind, the two boys mope while the girls bustle around feeding Edward's rabbit and indulging in other memorial acts, little anticipating, as the narrator points out, how changed and scornful of their present efforts this "Ulysses" will be when he next returns to them from "Troy."

The story when it originally appeared did not enlarge upon this change and its significance, but, in the book form, Grahame added a long passage. The narrator goes on to draw a moral from the girls' fruitless activity, one that further hammers in the idea of childhood as a point in time when one is mercifully shielded from "a glimpse into futurity" (*G,* 251). Finally, the narrator points out—giving this observation an additional and characteristically ironic twist—even long after we have passed childhood we perhaps are unable to judge the worth of our activities, having little capacity at any time to determine how much of what we do is "solid achievement" and how much "the merest child's play" (*G,* 252). The reader is forced here to enter into the ambivalence of this double vision where child's play is attractive, yet doomed, while what looks like the solid achievement of adulthood may be no different.

Stevenson writes, in his essay "Child's Play," that "The regret that we have for our childhood is not wholly justifiable."[12] He sees adult-hood as a time when the mature imaginative faculty is enlarged and flexible, while Grahame, in his depiction of Olympians in *The Golden Age*, suggests that only the capacity to return almost literally to child's play will preserve the imagination, developed to its *greatest* ca-pacity in childhood. Although in his late essay, "Oxford Through a Boy's Eyes," Grahame manages to depict the exciting challenge of go-ing away to school, here, taking the boy's point of view, he pictures going away to school as an end and not a beginning; it becomes a time when, as Wordsworth claims in his "Ode: Intimations of Immor-tality," "Shades of the prison house begin to close / Upon the grow-ing Boy." In *The Golden Age* as a whole, Grahame depicts little in adult life as sustaining and nurturing to the imagination except the memories and celebration of the golden age of childhood.

Chapter Five

Projecting the Future in *Dream Days*

Critics tend to read and study *The Golden Age* and *Dream Days* as one book, as if the latter were simply a continuation of the earlier stories; stories are taken out of either collection and treated individually, disregarding context. The two collections are indeed similar in that the second makes no more effort than the first to become a novel with developing characters or plot, nor has the narrative stance or general philosophy of the relationship between children and adults changed materially. Also like *The Golden Age* stories, the first six of the *Dream Days* pieces were published initially in periodicals: Henley's *New Review* (successor to the *National Observer*), the *Yellow Book,* and the American *Scribner's Magazine*.

One rather obvious difference between the two collections results in subtle differences of tone and emphasis, however. Both books are approximately the same length, yet the first is made up of eighteen separate pieces and the second of only eight. Thus, most of the pieces in *Dream Days* are considerably longer than their predecessors, and one, "The Reluctant Dragon," is four or five times the length of the typical *Golden Age* story. The second book seems less episodic than the first. Leisureliness of description and digression is highly developed in *Dream Days,* giving it a quality that fits well with the title, as does the fact that in at least four of the central stories the narrator has elaborate fantasies in which he projects himself into both the future and exotic places. All of these central fantasies involve girls and women either comically or romantically. While these pieces pick up on traits already exhibited in "Young Adam Cupid," "The Finding of the Princesses," and "The Roman Road," the solitary daydream has center stage as it does not in the earlier stories.

Adults have less place here than they did in *The Golden Age.* They are still powerful agents of conformity and punishment, condemned for their indifference and insensitivity, with some outstanding examples of Olympian goodness, yet Grahame moves away from the heavy emphasis on adult-child relations that prevails in *The Golden Age*. Moreover, relationships among the siblings fade into the background. The familial is played down in *Dream Days;* less embedded in the family scene, the narrator stands out. This change in emphasis is suggestive of two types of development, one on the part of Grahame, the man himself, moving in sophisticated literary circles in London and enjoying being an adult, and the other projected upon the narrator as boy, now assuming Edward's place in the family and looking forward ambivalently but certainly not entirely negatively to a move out into the wider world.

"The Twenty-First of October"

The first of these *Dream Days* stories plunges right in, with no prologue, assuming a familiarity with character and setting. From this first story, one would also not be able to predict the heavy emphasis on the narrator and on daydreaming exhibited by the central stories in this volume.

Selina is featured here as a young woman with an obsessive mission: to celebrate "Trafalgar Day" in such a way as best to honor the memory of her long-time hero, Admiral Lord Nelson, on the anniversary of his historic sea battle. Selina accomplishes her mission when all the others, both adults and children, are elsewhere, save Harold, whom she enlists to find fuel for an enormous bonfire, mainly by raiding the gardener's supplies. This bonfire, over which Selina presides like some ancient priestess, is indeed magnificent—almost worth the punishment and deprivation of privileges that follow.

The introduction to this piece—which shares elements of a satire on conventional education with many works of the period for both adults and children—puts Selina's strange obsession with Nelson into context. The narrator depicts the children as unenthusiastic and dull at ingesting the arbitrary, rote curriculum forced on them, but surprisingly inspired and thorough in dealing with subjects that excite their fancy. The three older children, in particular, have their chosen fields of study on which they are as "up" as any modern child with a special hobby. Edward's is the British army, Selina's, the British navy, and the narrator's, the Wild West. Thus Selina's October twenty-first bonfire becomes a natural extension of an innate curiosity and imaginative enthusiasm that most Olympians have lost and which they are generally incapable of sparking in their educational charges.

"Dies Irae"

Even in the midst of these dream days occurs for the child as well as the adult what the narrator hyperbolically entitles a "day of wrath" (using one of the traditional Latin labels for Judgment Day); such days are, he explains, "blind with the spatter of a misery uncomprehended, unanalyzed . . ." (*D*, 25).

As in "Exit Tyrannus," the child—in this case the narrator very specifically—is affected by glimpses of adult vulnerability and self-centeredly aggrieved by them. On this day of wrath, the sympathetic housemaid receives the news that her sailor brother (known and liked by the children) has been drowned at sea: "Martha was miserable and—and I couldn't get a new bootlace" (*D*, 27). Moreover, Selina and Charlotte are despondent and will not play because Edward has not acknowledged gifts they sent in the latest school parcel; Harold complains of a sore knee when the narrator begins an aggressive game with him.

Solitary wandering and daydream are the only things for it. The sight of a settlement of lay religious brothers, where the narrator has been previously entertained by the inhabitants, evokes in him an ascetic daydream of an orderly simple life, monastic to the point of self-flagellation—a life so self-sacrificing that it would cause his relatives to recognize how ill they had appreciated him in his past secular existence and to beg his forgiveness. Interrupted in his masochistic daydream by a clod of dirt thrown by the gardener's boy, "a red prolitariat, who hated me because I was a gentleman" (*D*, 40), the narrator turns his hostility in this direction, working off his frustration in a fight in which he routs both the enemy and his own bad spirits. He returns home to find his siblings in a much better mood. A letter has arrived from Edward. Martha, red-eyed but kind and thoughtful, serves the children an enormous tea. The narrator as a boy has by this time so satisfied his own needs that he cannot figure out why Martha has then to go to her own room and lock herself in.

Not only does this story show the insensitivity of children to adult suffering, an insensitivity on which Stevenson remarks in "Child's Play" and Grahame depicts elsewhere, but it interestingly suggests that the narrator is beginning to take on Edward's role in the family in more ways than one—moving toward the day when he, too, will enter into the aggressive hurly-burly of a boy's school and street life. His bullying approach to Harold is like that of Edward in "Snow-bound"; both his mood-cleansing fight with the gardener's boy and his self-pitying daydream have a Tom-Sawyerish quality, although the expression of class differences in his fight is clearly British.

"Mutabile Semper"

Reminiscent too of some of Tom Sawyer's difficulties with Becky Thatcher is the narrator's encounter in this story with a young woman of the "always changeable" rather than "forever faithful" variety. The narrator is nothing loath to converse with the new girl in town whom he is pleased to find on the other side of her garden fence as he takes a note to the parsonage. In their conversation, the young woman manages to entice him into revealing the daydream he has been having about a secret place—the sort of place where "if you want anything at all, you've only *got* to want it, and you can have it" (*D,* 51). In atmosphere, if not architecture, this place is much like the city projected in "The Roman Road." But the young woman is not as compatible a listener as the Artist. As the details emerge of boating on a river and arriving at a palace which includes a "chocolate room," the girl insists upon controlling both the narrator and the details of the dream. She thus reveals herself as an incipient controlling female Olympian, who, for instance, demands "You must give *me* all the chocolate, and then I'll give *you*—I'll give you what you ought to have" (*D,* 54). In spite of other warnings of her tendencies, which may lean toward the treacherous as well as the domineering, the smitten narrator agrees to meet with her that afternoon, a meeting delayed by rain.

As usual, bad weather forces the siblings at home upon each other; in the present circumstances, another domineering female, Selina, insists upon interfering with both the narrator's painting and Harold's writing of a "death-letter"—a kind of last will and testament, which is included in its entirety in the text, adding to our picture of Harold as the one with the quirky imagination. These familial incidents, which might in themselves have constituted an entire story in *The Golden Age,* here form a digressive, if thematically supportive, interlude in the real business of the story, which is to have the narrator find out how truly unfaithful his new love is.

The narrator, full of imaginary offerings for her, returns to her garden when the rain has cleared, only to find her involved with another boy. Neither responds to his greeting. After the initial rude shock, the narrator feels a renewed sense of freedom: "quit of all female whims and fanciful restrictions" (*D,* 68). He has escaped seductive wiles similar to those Grahame outlines for the unwary male in his *Pagan Papers* essay, "The Fairy Wicket."

"The Magic Ring"

The next story begins with a "text" on which Grahame enlarges throughout the first part of "The Magic Ring": "Grown-up people really ought to be more careful" (*D,* 71). The thoughtlessness of the Olympians affords the occasion for this story (although grown-ups are in part redeemed by the events). Relatives first suggest taking the children to the circus, allowing them thus to build "their star-pointing alhambras" (*D,* 71) upon this shaky ground. Then, sure enough, on the alloted day, it turns out that the adults are going to a garden party instead.

Harold and the narrator, who are featured in this story, react in their characteristic ways—the former by howling, the latter by retreat into nature and daydream. After fighting each other, the two unite to throw stones at passerbys. Fortunately, the first of the latter, in his dog cart, is another of those blessed Olympians who has managed somehow to carry his imagination intact into adulthood. He is already known to the children as "the funny man" because of his ability to discern their needs and desires. Using his unfailing instinct for "some magnificently luminous suggestion that cleared every cloud away" (*D,* 83), the funny man suggests that the three of them go off to the circus. He acknowledges that he too has a difficult home situation: he wishes to escape both his wife and the visiting curate.

With Harold singing "the great spheral circus song," which includes—at least to the narrator's enchanted ears—a paean to "The Woman of the Ring" (*D,* 86), they are off. They are soon to see this very woman in considerably more flesh than they are accustomed to. Both Harold and the narrator are at first overwhelmed by her embodiment in the fair Coralie, clothed in pink and spangles, and then swept away by the vision of Zephryine, "The Bride of the Desert," in black. The narrator is momentarily distracted by the clown, whose profession seems ideal to him, but is mainly seduced by these visions of womanhood so contrary to his everyday sight of woman as "a drab thing, hour-glass shaped, nearly legless, bunched here, constricted there" (D, 88). His daydreams about the horseback-riding females take the form of flight with first one and then the other to exotic lands. Zephyrine's dusky charms win out in these visions, with some passing regret for Coralie.

These glittering women on horseback—who both contrast so clearly with the relatives left behind, either garden-partying in "mauve tulle" (D, 74–75) or taking tea with the curate—reveal the narrator's taste for the exotic. The choice of Zephyrine in particular rings erotically adultlike, and can perhaps be attributed more to Grahame himself as a man in his thirties than to a preadolescent boy. Yet the reaching out beyond the narrow family world to strange lands and foreign princesses, a reaching out that will occur in the next two stories as well, may also be seen as a move toward adolescence in the developing boy. At any rate, for either man or boy the wishfulfilling daydream with its exotic and erotic elements, romantic or escapist as it may be, is still more future-oriented than a nostalgic longing to return to or remain in a family-oriented, static golden age of childhood.

"Its Walls Were as of Jasper"

Taking its title from the description of Jerusalem as a heavenly, walled, engemmed city, in the New Testament Book of Revelation, this story is one of the most original in both collections of tales, although its central imaginative component—the idea of actually entering a picture one is contemplating—is somewhat reminiscent of Alice's crossing into the Looking Glass world of Carroll's sequel to Wonderland. In "The Walls Were as of Jasper," the imaginative capacities of the children go far beyond the limits Stevenson sets for them in "Child's Play."

The story begins by describing the children's habit of alloting characters in picture books among themselves, giving each child a personal interest, "in a particular member of the cast, whose successes and rebuffs one took as so much private gain or loss" (D, 97). This habit is extended and transformed by both Charlotte and the boy narrator in regard to not only the characters in a picture hanging on the dining room wall, but to the background setting of this picture, which includes meadowland and a winding road on which knights ride two-by-two up to a walled city on a hill overlooking a harbor.

Both the narrator and Charlotte have separately tried to ascend this road in their imaginations and enter the city, but have felt barred from it. Charlotte has, however, contrived the ingenious method of imagining herself atop the crow's nest of a ship in the harbor, looking over the wall.

The narrator is miffed at Charlotte's superior progress into the world of the picture, but has the opportunity to best her on an enforced visit with Aunt Eliza to a house where, wandering off from the ladies, he finds a library that seems another of those satisfying rooms like the Rector's study in "A Harvest." This library also boasts a magnificent volume full of color pictures of just such a walled city as the dining-room picture, but the pictures here take the boy inside the walls to an event that appears to be a wedding. He settles himself down with the lavishly illustrated book on the hearth rug, using the coal shuttle to hold the pages down, and imagines himself in his "own little city" (*D*, 111) joining in the festivities, whose other guests, including several angels, are described in detail. He has reached the point of accompanying the bridal party on their trip to "the happy island" (*D*, 117) where they will all dine together, when his dreams are rudely interrupted by Aunt Eliza's arrival; she suddenly grabs her errant nephew by the scruff of his neck. As he is hauled home in disgrace, he takes a leaf out of Harold's book and maintains "a diplomatic blubber" the entire way, in order to be left to dream in peace of setting out for the little walled town "When I've grown up big and have money of my own and a full-sized walking stick" (*D*, 119). This blatant dream of adult male potency transcends the humiliating position in which the boy now finds himself.

Like the bureau which appears in "The Secret Drawer," the book of pictures featured in this story comes from Grahame's own adult life and acquired tastes for antique furniture and Italian primitive painting. Grahame himself identified the pictures of the town as a composite from several coveted books of the time.[1] He demonstrates here a masterly ability to weave these evocative pictures into a boyish daydream that ignores the boundaries of time and space. In so doing, Grahame goes well beyond the pastoral uses of place that were usually associated with his writing after the publication of *The Wind in the Willows*. This and other images of dream cities that he projects in these collections, with their mixed medieval and apocalyptic associations, deserve fuller examination than they have hitherto received. Significantly, the child's past contact with nature as some lost Garden

of Eden is not featured here. Instead, the man-made bustling city,
celebrating a wedding, forms the paradisial image—romantic, but
in some important ways again distinctly future rather than past
oriented.[2]

"A Saga of the Seas"

Grahame, in "The Magic Ring," develops a boyish image of
grown-up pleasures and privileges: "Life lies at their feet, a party-
coloured india-rubber ball; they may kick it this way or kick it that,
it turns up blue, yellow, or green, but always coloured and glisten-
ing" (D, 71). "A Saga of the Seas" brings out more clearly some of
the anxieties about women, adult relationships, and the demands of
society that underlie, however, the *Dream Day* visions of the brilliant
self-indulgence available to adults.

At the beginning of this story, the boy narrator finds himself, playing with tin soldiers, on the floor of the drawing room when some
ladies come to call. Ignoring him, they talk at length about their
grievances against "Men in general and Man in particular" (D, 123).
The latter is seriously indicted for lack of "tact, considerateness and
right appreciation" (D, 124), a charge that the boy then levels at one
of the ladies herself when she knocks over a line of soldiers with her
skirt and fails to apologize or help set them aright. Sent off to the
"St. Helena of the nursery" (D, 124) for his rudeness, this would-be
Napolean remembers a game of rafts the children had played that
morning in a "round spongebath on a bald deal towel-horse placed
flat on the floor." Stepping into the rocking of the spongebath, the
boy sets off in his imagination on "a full-blooded voyage of the Man,
equipped and purposeful, in search of what was his rightful own" (D,
126). His ensuing daydream is vividly detailed from the preparations
for voyage, through the ship's sail to first frigid and then tropical
zones, and its eventual victory over a pirate ship.

The captain of this victorious vessel then makes his rightful claim
to a Princess "carried off to be sold in captivity to the bold bad
Moors, and now with beating heart awaiting her rescue by . . . the
Perseus of her dreams" (D, 135). After the usual civilities, the Princess and the captain agree "to be fast friends" and they show each
other their treasures—an exchange of which Freud might make much.
The captain's offering is his latest knife, hers "a musical box with a
glass top that let you see the works . . ." (D, 136) and various other

equally suggestive toys. The two friends dine with the captain of a British man-of-war that has lain along side applauding but not aiding in the recent battle; then they retire to the cabin, where they lock the door and play games with these suggestive toys.[3]

But this is not yet a completed vision of "happily ever after." The imaginary voyage continues with the captain finding that he does not have much time for the Princess as he goes about the other exciting business of the sea voyage: capturing a French ship and dispensing mercy to its captain. The voyage home and the return are triumphant. The captain rides up the main street of his town with the princess at his side; the ringing of bells stands for both his triumph and the realization that it is time for tea in the schoolroom. As the erstwhile captain descends the stairs he hears the aggrieved ladies just leaving: "Man was still catching it apparently—Man was getting it hot. And much man cared! The seas were his and the islands . . . and there were Princesses in plenty waiting for him somewhere—Princesses of the right sort" (*D*, 146).

As in *The Headswoman*, in "The Saga of the Seas" the power of women and their ability to enforce society's rules is first unveiled and then surmounted in an ameliorating way—playful, yet implicitly erotic. In "The Walls were as of Jasper," the boy has looked forward to the wedding trip that he imagines himself taking in order to learn from it "*how* people lived happily every after. We would all go together, He and She, and the angels and I . . . and then the story would really begin" (*D*, 116). In "The Saga of the Seas," the games played behind the locked door of the captain's cabin between "fast friends" are a happy vision of wedded bliss as well. The question of female power is temporarily forgotten, while the captain is confidently in control and master of the seas and the islands. Here, as elsewhere in Grahame's writing, the sea seems to stand for freedom from a landlocked society. Yet a key to Grahame's conflicts about women and their role in adult life is buried beneath the surface of this story in the narrator's description of himself as the Perseus of Greek myth, who must kill Medusa and establish his power over her two Gorgon sisters before he can hope to win his Princess, Andromeda.

"The Reluctant Dragon"

As he will later do in *The Wind in the Willows*, Grahame adopts in the story within a story of "The Reluctant Dragon" a less complicated and ambivalent evocation of the pleasures of adult life by making his principal characters grown-up unmarried males, or, in the case of the boy in "The Reluctant Dragon," singularly free of Olympian restraint.

This long tale of a boy, a sociable dragon, and an accommodating St. George (discussed in detail in chapter three) was only much later taken out of the context of *Dream Days* and published separately. Its original story is embedded in the tale of Charlotte and the boy narrator's finding mysterious footprints in the snow and, deciding that they are dragon prints, following them practically to the doorstep of the man whom the children call "the funny man," first introduced in "The Magic Ring." The funny man entertains them graciously and then walks them home, yielding on the way to Charlotte's plea for a story. The congeniality of this good Olympian walking home in the dusk with the youngsters is reflected in the story of good fellowship that he tells: where the intelligent boy, in perfect accord with his humble, indulgent parents, manages to arrange for a mock fight between a sociable, poetic dragon and a correct but flexible St. George, ending in a great village celebration with the dragon, the drunken hit of the evening, assisted home by his two friends.

Like *The Wind in the Willows* too, the tale of "The Reluctant Dragon" has both outlasted *The Golden Age* and *Dream Days* and achieved popularity among children. Its appeal for the child might be found in the difference between the tale and its narrational frame. Although the narrator of *Dream Days* and "the funny man" tell stories in about the same way—in a conversational tone, alternating between sophisticated exposition and description and colloquially rendered conversation—the weight in the tale itself has shifted toward dialogue. Moreover, its descriptive and expository passages are not heavy with allusions and quotations as they often tend to be in *The Golden Age* and *Dream Days,* which to some extent follow the stylistic pattern of *Pagan Papers.* The funny man's awareness of a child audience determines this difference in stylistic density. The ensuing lightness of tone, accompanied by a substantive shift in power to those characters with whom a child reader might readily identify, makes the funny man's tale more attractive to the child than is the general run of stories about these orphaned siblings.

The question of power is a crucial one. While here the funny man is exceedingly gracious, nevertheless, in story after story, *The Golden Age* and *Dream Days* children are dependent upon the good will of the

Olympians; this good will is not always forthcoming and is sometimes proffered with a patronizing air. Children in these stories have little power or control over the forces either personal or impersonal (for example, growth and change) that rule their lives. But the fantasy situation presented in the inner tale of "The Reluctant Dragon" puts the Boy in a position of equality or better with all those around him. He comes home at bedtime, for instance, only as a courtesy to his mother, patronizes his parents for their lack of knowledge of "natural history and fairy tales," bullies the Dragon, and talks to St. George man to man. Since he helps to arrange and stage the fight between the Dragon and the Saint, he has a sense of control over its outcome. This tale can be read as a psychological allegory of successful integration of id, ego, and superego.[4] Read even at its most obvious level, the tale is clearly one of child-satisfying triumph.

In contrast, *The Golden Age* and *Dream Days* stories as a whole are realistic enough not only to depict few childhood triumphs but also to view the stage of childhood as fleeting. Through the retrospective narrator, with whom adult readers are likely to identify, these stories incorporate both a nostalgia for childhood and an irony about its loss alien to children themselves. The fantasy status of the story within a story, however, gives the tale of "The Reluctant Dragon" a universality with regard to place and a corresponding eternality with regard to time not characteristic of the collection as a whole. Although the tale of "The Reluctant Dragon" does not begin with the formulaic "Once upon a time," it approximates the fairy-tale beginning with "Long ago . . . in a cottage halfway between this village and yonder shoulders of the downs . . ." (*D*, 156). The ending portrays a "happy ever after" camaraderie. In this tale, the Boy need not grow up and go adventuring, nor face women and the demands of society, in order to assume power and control over his life.

"A Departure"

Like the last story in *The Golden Age*, "A Departure" is concerned with the end of an era in childhood, one that, like Edward's going away to school, is precipitated by the Olympians. In this case, however, the ending is taken over and ritualized by the children themselves.

The narrator begins with a long discussion of the ambivalent ways in which the children regard various forms of "inheritance," of clothes and the like, from their older siblings. He then narrows his focus to the passing down of toys, which are the more readily given up to younger siblings because they are then still available in moments of regression, "on wet afternoons" (D, 210). But there comes a time when even the youngest in families such as this, is, like Charlotte, considered "too matronly for toys" (D, 211). The change often comes without warning and consent. Here Uncle Thomas, in one of his enthusiasms, decides to pack up and give away all of the toys to the children's hospital. The narrator, Harold, and Charlotte, find themselves "indignant, betrayed, and sullen to the verge of mutiny" (D, 213).

Descriptions of various toys and their relationships to the children fill the next few pages. With loving detail, Grahame paints Leotard "an acrobat . . . who lived in a glass box" and revolves in various gyrations around a bar, "the spotty horse" on which they have "ridden" around the nursery on pretended glorious adventures, and the Noah's Ark with its various animals (D, 114–17). These fulsome descriptions remind us that Grahame was at the time amassing a toy collection for his adult enjoyment.

The narrator of "A Departure" notes, however, that at the time of the story he himself was already obsessed with catapults, so mainly merely nostalgic. Closer to the banished toys, Harold and Charlotte for the first time take matters into their own hands; they plan the mutiny without him. They awaken him in the middle of the warm June night for what turns out to be a solemn Midsummer's Eve festival in which they raid the box of toys in the school room, abstracting the doll Rosa and Potiphar, "a finely modelled bull with a suede skin, rough and comfortable and warm in bed" (D, 223). The two younger ones lead the narrator out into the "Moonlight" and "Post Ten o'clock Land" (D, 225) of the garden, where they hold a solemn funeral, burying the two honored sacrifices while "the Man in the Moon" smiles down upon them benignly—seeming to give blessing to this rite of passage.

Dream Days begins with the rather pagan ritual of the October twenty-first bonfire and ends on this similarly pagan note. As such, this ending seems more affirmative and ameliorative than does the ending of *The Golden Age,* which looks back with an ironic eye on all human activities as "child's play." As Green points out, the Man in the Moon, as he is briefly described by the narrator, is a guardian of the past and therefore of childhood itself; he also has definite artistic, or at least storytelling association.[5] He is one whom the narrator feels happy to leave "behind on the spot; a good fellow too, cherry, comforting, with a fund of anecdote; a man in whom one had every confidence" (*D*, 228). Like the Great God Pan, as depicted by Grahame in *The Wind in the Willows*, the Man in the Moon is a mythological figure—unorthodoxly portrayed in these works as having warmly paternal characteristics—who acts as an unthreatening constant in a world that may change for the worst.

Adulthood in *Dream Days*

In retrospect, one can see that during the period between 1895 and 1898, after the publication of *The Golden Age*, which met with such great literary esteem, and while he was writing the *Dream Days* stories, Grahame was enjoying the halcyon days of his adulthood. He was a financially secure bachelor; the doors of London were open to him; he had leisure for travel in Italy and vacations in Cornwall; he could begin collecting both adult toys—antique furniture and art books—and toys more usually associated with childhood. Both this fulfilling life-style and the exorcism of bitterness permitted by the writing of stories about childhood which are to some extent autobiographical seem reflected in the somewhat positive approach in *Dream Days* toward ideas of children's future growth and change.

The visions that the narrator has, as a boy, for himself as an adult, while admittedly daydreams fraught with considerable anxiety over the reality of sex and society, suggest, nevertheless, possibilities for interesting movement into the wide world, possibilities that previously seemed closed by the heavy nostalgia and pessimistic irony of *The Golden Age*. The fact that these daydreams are often associated with visions of cities, with their man-made complexities, rather than with the natural countryside, enhances one's sense that Grahame was reflecting his own wider view of the world in the narrator as a boy, with his tentative and hesitant movement toward the concerns of adolescence.

Even within that context, however, the story of "The Reluctant Dragon" can be seen as a harbinger of the direction that Grahame's thinking and writing will follow some ten years later, after he has taken more risks and made decisive life choices of marriage, family, and enhanced responsibilities at the Bank of England. For when those particular adult choices disappoint him, as they seem to have done, he will choose not only to move back to the pastoral setting of his childhood but also to write a novel, ostensibly for his son, that seems deliberately to eliminate the possibility of making such life choices. Grahame will ultimately, in *The Wind in the Willows,* reject the wide world—depicting its manifold attractive temptations as far too dangerous. He will make much of very simple, circumscribed pleasures enjoyed by a rural community of well-meaning males.

Chapter Six

The Mythological Present of *The Wind in the Willows*

Grahame's many readers waited nearly a decade for yet another sequel to the stories about the five *Golden Age* children. *The Wind in the Willows,* appearing in England in October 1908, disappointed them; the manuscript had also disappointed Grahame's English editor, John Lane, who would not chance it, and the American magazine, *Everybody's,* which, through Constance Smedley, had first solicited the new work. Methuen in England and Scribner's in America thus took a gamble, the latter at the urging of the recently won-over Teddy Roosevelt. This was a gamble neither publisher had reason to regret in later years.

Contemporary critics were not as lucky in the eyes of posterity. Their rather biting remarks about this "animal fable" show little perception of the true nature of the work and poor judgment about the standards to apply to it.[1] However, to give them sympathy if not credit, *The Wind in the Willows,* as a novel-length animal fantasy for children, had no clear generic predecessor on which they could lean. Although both had their influence on Grahame's work, Richard Jefferies's anthromorphizing tale, *Wood Magic* (1881), was far more clearly allegorical than Grahame's, as was Carroll's earlier *Alice's Adventures in Wonderland* (1865). Moreover, a child protagonist was central to these earlier books, as it was to Grahame's own "The Reluctant Dragon," while *The Wind in the Willows* shifted the identification of the reader to the animal characters themselves. The first adult readers of Grahame's *The Wind in the Willows* showed little adaptability to this identification, which seemed to come quite naturally, however, to the first child readers—tested as it were on Alastair Grahame, otherwise known as Mouse.

The Odyssean Plot and Structure

The plot of *The Wind in the Willows* is generally simple and easy to follow. The structure becomes only somewhat complex in the middle of the book when chapters begin to alternate between the experiences of the stay-at-home characters, Rat and Mole, and the adventures of Toad, who is out in what Grahame calls the Wide World.

One spring day Mole pops his head out of his hole and decides to abandon the spring cleaning of his underground home for a stroll along the riverbank. Here he meets the friendly Water Rat and is quickly introduced by him to the joys of "messing about in boats" and lavish picnics (chapter 1). Although Mole does not understand Rat's penchant for writing poetry, their friendship develops rapidly. Mole remains with his new friend for more than a year, learning river lore and meeting another river dweller, the rich and faddist Toad, owner of Toad Hall. The latter persuades them to hit the open road with him in his well-appointed gypsy caravan, drawn by a much protesting horse who finally upsets the contraption when forced off the road by a speeding, "poop-pooping" motor car. The car entrances Toad, who abandons the caravan without a backward glance; Rat and Mole are happy to get back home in one piece (chapter 2).

As the year goes on, Mole is anxious to explore more, including the area across the river known as the Wild Wood, inhabited by creatures considered unreliable by Rat, except for the gruff and rather unsociable Badger, who lives underground in its center. Exploring alone, Mole becomes lost and terrified; Rat finds him, but the two friends are endangered by an early snowstorm until they stumble upon Badger's doorstep and find refuge with him (chapter 3). Badger's underground hospitality is welcome and warming (chapter 4), just as is Mole's underground home when, later, close to Christmas, he and Rat wander back to it and Mole has the opportunity to become reacquainted with its charms. Reassured by its continued existence, he is able to leave his home once again (chapter 5).

Meanwhile, however, Toad has been indulging in his motorcar mania, wrecking car after car. When he wakes from his winter nap, Badger, who takes a paternal interest in Toad, the son of a dead friend, insists that Rat and Mole must help him to "persuade" Toad to reform. They do this finally by locking him into his bedroom and guarding him. Through trickery, Toad escapes, finds another motor car to steal, is caught, tried, convicted, and sentenced to jail for twenty years (chapter 6). While Toad is gone, Rat and Mole have several other experiences together; the first is a mystical one when they go searching for the lost son of Otter, Portly, and, late on a summer night, find him on an island in the middle of a weir, under the protection of Pan, the nature god (chapter 7).

Toad, jailed and in despair, nevertheless develops some semblance of his old self under the ministrations of the sympathetic jailer's daughter, who also arranges for him to escape in the clothing of her aunt, the jail's washerwoman. His escape is much complicated by this disguise, although he uses it upon occasion to gain sympathy. First going to a railway station, he finds himself without money and papers. He prevails upon the engine driver, however, to take him on. When they are chased by another engine bearing the forces of law and order, Toad manages, with the connivance of the engine driver, to jump from the train (chapter 8).

During this period, Rat, back at home, also experiences wanderlust when he sees all of his friends packing to go south for the winter. A passing Sea Rat enchants him with tales of far-off places and almost persuades him to come along. Mole has forceably to restrain him and return his attention to writing poetry (chapter 9).

Toad, still in washerwomen's clothes, is having further adventures trying to get home; he hitches a ride on a barge from which he is thrown off by the bargewoman when he cannot wash her clothes; he steals the barge horse and trades it to a Gypsy for pocket money and a meal; he is picked up by and attempts once more to steal the same motorcar he stole before. He finally is chased into the river, from which he is hauled out at Rat's doorstep (chapter 10).

All the main characters come together again at this point in order to help Toad regain possession of Toad Hall, which in his absence, despite the efforts of his friends, has been taken over by weasels, stoats, and ferrets, the untrustworthy inhabitants of the Wild Woods. Under Badger's direction, the four animals plan a successful invasion through underground passages, rout the false inhabitants, cleanse the hall, and enjoy a triumphal banquet. Throughout, Toad is forced to take a modest backseat, despite his efforts to dominate at each stage of the affair and then his exhibitionist plans for the banquet. The book ends with this gala celebration of the somewhat dubious reformation of Toad and the maintenance of the status quo effected by his good friends (chapters 11–12).

Even given in the above detail, the plot may seem simpler and more trivial than it appears upon careful examination. Beneath its surface is a unity and subtle thematic structure that have fooled some readers even up to the present day; they describe the novel too facilely as episodic. Such readings assume that Grahame was still writing as he did about the five children in his previous two books. He was not. In various ways, over these years of relative silence, Grahame acquired a sense of total form that he did not exhibit in any of the three earlier works and only previously mastered in the relatively short *The Headswoman* and "The Reluctant Dragon."

To some extent, this sense of form was already built into the story in its first written manifestation, the letters that Grahame sent to his son during their periods away from each other from early May through September of 1907.[2] With certain notable exceptions, these fifteen letters preserved by Miss Stott, Alastair's governess, feature Toad's adventures in outline much as they appear in the book in chapters 6, 8, and 10–12. They provide the basic outline of the mock-epic plot of *The Wind in the Willows,* with Toad taking the part of a mock Odysseus or Ulysses in his journey back to a home which has been invaded by alien presences and must be cleansed of them. (These invaders, of course, replace the Odyssean suitors in a world without the faithful Odyssean wife, Penelope.) When writing the book, Grahame made perfectly clear the allusion to the Odyssey in the title of its last chapter—"The Return of Ulysses"—and, in a number of more subtle ways, stylistic and otherwise, echoes the Greek poem. Moreover, although in the case of the taking of the hall Badger and Mole seem to be the ones who display the military strategy for which Ulysses was famous, Toad's essential character, even at his most comical, is like that of Ulysses in one trait that has also been emphasized by classical scholars: that is, Ulysses is a trickster. Throughout his misadventures, Toad, like Ulysses with Cyclops and others, is a successful con man.

Grahame adopts also the traditional twelve-part epic structure, including within its boundaries many other incidents that do not affect or include Toad in any way. This is because Toad, colorful as he is and clearly beloved of the child audience, is not the only Odyssean protagonist. Those who ignore the parts played by Rat and Mole in particular fail to grasp the totality of the book. For this and other reasons, A. A. Milne's theatrical adaptation, *Toad of Toad Hall,* for example, successful as it may be as a play, fails to do justice to the novel. The special quality that holds the book together and knits the beginning of the book thematically with its ending is Grahame's stripping down of the Odyssean adventure to a certain bare essential meaningful to him personally—the search for one's true home—and his repeating it for three main characters—Mole, Rat, and Toad. He ignores the incidents involving Penelope. Yet at the same time, partly through the adventure of the little otter Portly, he manages to highlight the Telemachan aspect of the Odyssey, the unfortunate separation of father (Ulysses) and son (Telemachus). The structure of *The Wind in the Willows* is, therefore, composed of variations on the Odyssean theme of departure from and return to home: one strongly accented motif in the development of this theme is the relationship between fathers and sons; one repressed motif is the relationship between husbands and wives.

The Dominance of Space and Season

In order to examine adequately Grahame's development of this theme one must pay particular attention to his use of setting and time, or, more specifically, space and season. The playwright Graham Robertson, Grahame's friend and one-time London neighbor, once overheard Grahame saying to his wife, "You *like* people. They interest you. I am interested in *places!*"[3] Grahame certainly proves himself too much a master of character to be taken as unobservant of people. Yet his interest in place in both life and literature is unusually strong, even for one so influenced by the English romantics. Not nature alone but all types of settings, interior and exterior, take a foreground rather than a background position in his work, influencing and supporting the thematic structure and the nature of character development itself in *The Wind in the Willows*.

The work of Gaston Bachelard, who, in a book called *The Poetics of Space,* examines literary images of space in the poetry of Baudelaire and Rilke, can provide key terms for what Grahame seems to be expressing in his declaration, "I am interested in *places!*"[4] Bachelard describes such a stance as "topophilic" (partaking of love [Greek *philia*] of place [Greek *topos*]), and claims that a display of such topophilia in a work of art is usually associated with remembrance and evocation of a "felicitious space," often taken from early childhood. In Bachelard's terms, felicitous space is found in a place, interior or exterior, where one feels secure enough to allow one's imagination freely and safely to roam and play without fear of being psychically stifled or physically endangered.

Grahame implied such an affinity for the Mount, Cookham Dene—

the large house and the surrounding Berkshire countryside, with its
river and downs—when he spoke to Constance Smedley about those
years that were largely spent there. He said of the years when he was
four to seven years old that they were formative in the development
of his consciousness.[5] Two of these years were spent in Cookham
Dene, to which he returned in 1906. This setting gave him, at least
for the duration of its composition, the imaginative freedom to shape
and complete his masterpiece of topophilia. He obviously felt that he
had somehow succeeded in finding here his true home, from which
he had departed so long ago. He celebrated this return in the variations on the Odyssean pattern in *The Wind in the Willows,* examining
over and over again various images of felicitous space and his characters' changing relationships to them.

Grahame does this partly by having Rat, in a discussion with Mole
in the first chapter of the book, distinguish what he considers to be
felicitous space in the simplified geography that he projects. Three
divisions of space exist in Rat's mind: the River and its Bank, the
Wild Wood on one side of it, and the Wide World that surrounds
both. As far as Rat is concerned, only the first is truly felicitous
space, for the River to him is "brother and sister . . . and aunts, and
company and food and drink, . . . It's my world, and I don't want
any other. What it hasn't got is not worth having, and what it
doesn't know is not worth knowing" (*W,* 10). The Wild Wood, in
contrast, is filled by untrustworthy creatures and, to Rat, the Wide
World simply "doesn't matter" (*W,* 11). This particular division of
felicitous and infelicitous space is essentially confirmed by the de-
velopments in the book, although not without some serious ques-
tioning.

Like Charles Dickens in *Our Mutual Friend* and Mark Twain in
Huckleberry Finn, Grahame takes the image of the river, which has archetypal associations with the flow of life and time itself, and emphasizes those aspects of it that will best confirm the particular view of
life he means to convey (quite a different view from that of either
Dickens or Twain). In *The Wind in the Willows,* this means ignoring
what is actually happening along the Thames, already polluted in
Grahame's day, and envisioning the water as pure and life-enhancing
(only occasionally invaded in a rather jolly way by a bottle thrown off
a pleasure boat). This river provides not only all of life's necessities
but most of its pleasures, both physical and emotional. The River is
clearly considered to be imagination-enhancing, like all of the felici-

tous space that Bachelard recognizes. Rat's poetry is inspired by it. Almost immediately, Mole, not at all the poet, also senses this quality in his first exhilarating encounter with the River. By page 4, Mole is "bewitched, entranced, fascinated. By the side of the River he trotted as one trots, when very small, by the side of a man who holds one spellbound by exciting stories; and when tired at last, he sat on the bank, while the river still chattered on to him, a babbling procession of the best stories in the world, sent from the heart of the earth to be told at last to the insatiable sea" (*W*, 4).

Such bodies of water are archetypically associated with females and maternity, but Grahame, as can be seen from the description of Mole's enchantment, firmly establishes his own *paternal* theme in association with the river. This theme is further developed in chapter 7 in the scene with Pan, a scene that suggests that some space can be too marvelous to be felicitous, at least in Bachelard's terms. When Rat first outlines his revealing geography, he is unaware that an island exists in the middle of the Weir, an island on which Pan resides. Rat's and Mole's discovery of the island, while helping Otter search for his lost son Portly, provides each with his own characteristic epiphany and vision of a heavenly home for which neither earthly creatures is yet ready. Young Portly, meanwhile, has an experience of a heavenly father who is only standing in temporarily for his own father waiting anxiously at home for him.

Portly's sojourn on the island is a death that has no sting, but the space seen here, secure and beautiful as it is, is not immediately desirable: Grahame (unlike some early writers for children) is not ready to send his childlike characters to their heavenly home prematurely. In addition, the inspiration the Piper at the Gates of Dawn (as he names Pan in the chapter heading) and his music afford is too ethereal to be conveyed in earthly poetry. Rat, therefore, although the most affected by the vision, will be able to remember it no more than will Mole or Portly, and will continue to find his inspiration in the River and its mundane life, just as Portly will be satisfied with his good-enough father, Otter.

What makes this mundane life pleasant rather than boring is that Grahame's characters first of all do not have to grub for their livings. These small woodland creatures do not represent farmhands who toil from morning to night for their bread. Like such rural workers, however, they are allowed to live by a pastoral clock in a world whose modernity is signaled largely (and perhaps fatally) by the motor car.

Time, like the River, flows past in the book, marked not by hours and obligations but by diurnal and seasonal rhythmns. The characters take the best they can out of a pastoral world, where daytime activity and nighttime rest, summertime boating and picnicking outdoors, wintertime dozing and telling stories by the fire are made equally appealing. Contentment with diurnal and seasonal rhythmns is enhanced by the depiction of evening and winter as the times in which emotion can be recollected in tranquillity and imagination transposed into art; these are the times when images of felicitous space take shape in "river stories" and the like (*W*, 21).

With this emphasis on imaginative recreation comes a concomitant emphasis on the domestic space that shields the storytellers from the dark and the cold. Interiors are examined minutely for anthropomorphic details of comfort, reminding us of the narrator's consuming interest in arrangements of the Rector's study in Grahame's *Golden Age* story, "The Harvest." Beyond this, however, four major domiciles are contrasted: Badger's elaborate and ancient underground home; Mole's modest abode, just under the surface of the earth; the accessible riverbank dwelling of Rat; and the elaborate ancestoral mansion inherited by Toad.

While the elderly and stubbornly unchanging Badger seems to have found a perfect and stable match in his dwelling, each of the three major protagonists has a crisis in some way associated with his home and how close it comes to satisfying his personal needs.[6] In the depiction of these crises one can discern a major tension that seems to arise from Grahame's underlying recognition, if not direct admission, of the fact that finding a true home may force the individual psyche into an uneasy compromise between an individual's need for security and tranquillity and his often conflictual need for freedom and adventure, a need that cannot always be satisfied by the imagination. From those whose need for adventure is high, even the relatively free and little onerous domesticity lauded here can exact a psychic toll that may be the opposite of truly felicitous.

Character Development and Conflict

The degree to which the characters in this work are realistically delineated as animals, except in name, is debatable. Grahame's anthropomorphizing goes much farther than that of his contemporary, Beatrix Potter, for instance. She may dress Peter Rabbit up in a jacket, but sends him out to steal vegetables, not motor cars, an adventure quite in keeping with his rabbit nature. In addition, Potter strictly observes realistic scale in both her drawings and the interaction of her characters with natural or man-made objects.

In contrast, one can observe from the beginning of *The Wind in the Willows* that Grahame's Mole is not blind and that Grahame in his writing takes no pains to scale Rat's rowboat or his picnic basket to size (causing problems for his illustrators). These objects seem the very accoutrements of a creature whose nature is that of a gentleman poet and intellectual of independent means—which is what Rat is. Grahame could certainly have depicted his animals more naturalistically had he so wished. He nevertheless did not choose to limit himself in this way, achieving results that suggest that he was really more interested in people, even people with problems, than in animals or nature per se.

While all of the four major characters in *The Wind in the Willows* are ostensibly animals, they are also ostensibly adult. Those who are familiar with Grahame's earlier writing will recognize that these grown-up animals, Rat and Mole in particular, bear some resemblance in manner to the imaginative, childlike men—the Rector, the Artist, the funny man—whom Grahame created earlier; good, courteous fellows, often dreamers, still always ready to participate in those activities that are of interest to children. More clearly, however, than these exemplary Olympians, the animal characters are burdened by neither sexual longings nor professional ambitions. Moreover, the animals are free from the immediate domestic restraints that Grahame envisions as hampering either children or adults: parents, aunts and uncles, wives, domineering housekeepers, and stingy relatives. The animals also have no adult need to work for a living and submit to the other restraints that work entails. They thus live in a state of idyllic grace, relieved of many animal and human limitations. Yet Grahame also makes it clear, both explicitly and implicitly, that the major animal characters also live within a narrow range of the class system governing British social relationships in Grahame's day.

Mole, Rat, and Toad are created as recognizable middle-class types, ranging from lower middle-class to highest middle-class respectively. Badger's class is less certain; to some he seems close to an older breed of country squiredom, whose potential for antisocial gruffness and boasting ignorance or, alternatively, benevolent naiveté was immortalized by Fielding in the figures of Squire Western and Squire Allworthy in *The History of Tom Jones, A Foundling* (1749). To others, he seems more like an old family retainer. At any rate, all four of them own their own homes and, although the invisible hands of the servant class are never alluded to, even Mole, who seems to live under the most humble circumstances, can leave his spring-cleaning and return to find his house ship-shape. (When questioned in a letter about this seeming inconsistency, Grahame lightly suggested that a "char-mouse" had come to help out!)[7]

External conflict. The slight differences in class and wealth among the companions tend to enhance their companionship rather than cause conflict; none seems envious of another's characteristics or possessions. When one of their number is challenged in his position, as is Toad, they unite to defeat what amounts to an insurrection from the lower classes (as the inhabitants of the Wild Wood are clearly depicted) and to retain the inherited wealth of their less-than-responsible peer.

A major conflict among members of this band of friends does arise, however, over the refusal of Toad to adhere to the desired behavioral standards of his class. That conflict is played out in interesting ways. When Toad's waywardness, threatening to disgrace his family and class, comes to Badger's attention and the time is right, Badger moves in with more evangelistic fervor than was ever displayed by any of Grahame's human Olympians. In chapter 6, the moral suasion of admonitory sermons quickly gives way to physical restraints. Toad's friends, even Mole and Rat, do not hesitate to keep Toad prisoner in his own house. Mole uses similar physical restraints on Rat in chapter 9 to stop Rat from wandering away from his home. Apparently friends may behave violently toward each other in order to keep one of their number within the confines of the felicitous space established by Rat at the beginning.

On the surface of the story then, resolutions of these clashes of individual will, like the resolution of the fight over Toad Hall, favor those who restrain rather than those who rebel. Grahame, however, paints the middle-class rebels, Toad and Rat, in their wanderlust, as much more attractive than the inhabitants of the Wild Wood; he is also permissive toward Mole, whose restlessness is relatively confined. Thus, while Grahame's attitude toward class conflict is negative and unambivalent, his attitude toward individual rebellion is less clear. Characters' inner conflicts are certainly handled sympathetically, even if development and growth seem primarily directed toward very minor changes in circumstances, while general conformity and acceptance of one's place in life seem the desired goals.

Inner conflict. As a number of recent readers have remarked, of all the characters, Mole is the one who is permitted the most freedom for growth and development, growth that begins when he first pops out of his hole on that fateful spring day.[8] A whole new world opens up to him, and he takes advantage of it and is allowed to take advantage of it, going through a series of tests that begin with his hubristic upset of Rat's boat and end with his demonstration of military strategy as virtual second in command to Badger in the retaking of Toad Hall.

In the course of this testing, Mole too is punished for wandering out of his proper sphere. His trip into the Wild Wood on his own initiative, and his experience of the Terror of the Wild Wood—a trip that also reminds us of the obligatory trip of Odyssean heroes to Hell and back—is enough to prevent this epic hero from further solitary adventures. But Mole's experience on return to his own home is different from that of Rat and Toad. He alone of the three Odyssean protagonists is allowed to break out of the circle of departure and return.

One can only speculate about the reasons for Mole's greater freedom to leave home, return to it, and leave home again. Chapter 5, where Mole's return and new departure are acted out, calls attention to its concern with place in its Latin title, *"Dulce Domum"*—equivalent to "Home, Sweet Home." Mole certainly has a crisis of homesickness on the wintery day when he and Rat find themselves in the vicinity of Mole's End. He is pulled home not by his friend but by his own inner voices. Yet his one night at home is enough for him, filled as it is with recognition of all the familiar objects painstakingly gathered and cozy arrangements thoughtfully made, all of which Rat encourages him to explain. Even the feast that he and Rat manage to provide to Christmas-caroling field mice does not make him feel that he should remain. Mole wants to hang onto this place, but he recognizes it as "plain and simple . . . narrow even," and he wants also to return to the "upper world" and "the larger stage" (*W*, 103).

The degree of latitude permitted Mole is perhaps part of the carefully controlled balance that Grahame tries to achieve between security and adventure in the definition of felicitous space. In the previous chapter, Badger, sensing a fellow underground lover, has waxed eloquent to Mole on the virtues of the underground life, secure from the

hazards experienced by those who live on the edge of the River. Badger's home is large and ancient in a very special way. It is, according
to Badger, a sunken human city, long since abandoned by humans,
who "come and go" in a way that Badger scorns. However, Mole's
choice of above ground, his "new life and its splendid spaces" (W,
103), suggests that Badger's underground security is too restrictive.

The limited nature of Mole's home seems one reason why he is
granted relative freedom to leave it behind. Mole's character, temperament, even class position, also seem to make it possible to grant him
more freedom. Mole's modest need for adventure, so effectively controlled by his trip into the Wild Woods, is approved because it *is* so
modest. He is allowed also to develop his somewhat *limited* potential
precisely because it is limited, imaginatively and otherwise, and does
not threaten to get out of control. Indeed, Mole's potential can be
used to aid the forces of control in the external conflict between
Toad's colleagues and the intruders. Mole's development produces a
good second lieutenant out of a lower middle-class householder who
suddenly feels a longing for "higher things." Unlike the creatures of
the Wild Woods, whom he seems to know how to handle—using a
mixture of cunning, sternness, and camaraderie—Mole can be trusted
to remember and keep his own place—coming back to Mole's End in
the end.

Those who have a greater imagination or more money to spend
threaten more seriously to upset the balance between freedom and security in the felicitous space around the riverbank. Even Rat, who
seems by placement of his home and by temperament to appreciate
this balance, can be lured away from it by the force of his own imagination. In chapter 9, Mole forces Rat, who has previously participated
in the unsuccessful first attempt to control Toad, to recognize his
proper place and to sublimate his desire for adventure into the writing of poetry.

As his delineation of the geography would suggest, Rat is normally
a contented, rather cautious chap, happy with his life on the riverbank and quite willing to act as mentor to Mole, who, at first, seems
to respect everything about his new friend, except perhaps his tendency to wax poetic about ducks and other familiar creatures. Nevertheless, Rat can be tempted to follow the siren call of the Sea Rat,
who, dropping by on his way out to sea, tells such wonderful tales of
fun on ship and in port that Rat, acting nearly as obsessed as Toad
with the motor car, packs his satchel and takes off after his new ac-

quaintance. Mole, as ignorant as he may be of the sources of Rat's poetic urge, is yet able to recognize that one way he can turn Rat away from this new temptation is to force him to sit down with pencil and paper. Writing will reopen the channels of imagination through which Rat filters his experience of his own familiar felicitous space.

Chapter 9, called "Wayfarers All," a title that evokes the image not merely of travel, but of life as a pilgrimage, is perhaps the most ambiguous chapter of the whole book in terms of maintaining the delicate balance between security and adventure that Grahame fosters. The ending of the chapter, with Rat, apparently content, "absorbed and deaf to the world; alternatively scribbling and sucking the top of his pencil" (*W*, 188), rights the balance toward security. Grahame, nevertheless, makes the Sea Rat's call extremely attractive. He uses his own experience of Mediterranean port towns to add a note of authenticity to the description of the wandering life. Rat's vulnerability to the Sea Rat's stories is enhanced by his earlier conversations with his avarian neighbors, who are packing to go south, since it is fall. Their reactions to Rat's complaints of desertion paint an attractively natural picture of the biyearly urge to migrate from North to South and back again. The reasons why Rat should not share this migratory urge are not made entirely clear (Grahame at this point can hardly claim to be naturalistic). Should Rat not, like Mole, desire a "larger stage"? Apparently not. Mole is sure enough of this to wrestle with Rat and to lock him in; Rat's experience is, in the end, described as if it were a fit of insanity.

"Wayfarers All" is a curious chapter, into which, no doubt, Grahame poured much of his own longing for a less responsible, "Southern" life, expressed hitherto in essays like "The Long Odds." That essay, too, expresses his resolution to continue "the fight" on his own native ground. The sublimatory role of writing in this struggle between need for security and need for adventure is here made about as explicit as Grahame ever makes it: even space as felicitous as the riverbank can only be kept so in the imaginative mind by deliberate exercise of the imaginative faculty.

In Rat's case, this brief but violent departure and return, along with its opposite balancing extreme of the trip to the island in the middle of the Weir, constitutes his Odyssean journey. On both occasions, Rat is seduced through his ears, first by Pan's ethereal flute that lures him to a heavenly but static place and then by the Sea Rat's tales, which lure him to exotic and constant change. In the first case, Pan himself acts as a deafening agent and, in the second, Mole must assist Rat in figuratively tying himself to the mast of his everyday life, as Ulysses did to his boatmates in order not to heed the Siren call. The allusion to the Sirens helps buttress the ultimate decision made by both Rat (and Grahame himself) to stick to the River and Downs. Unlike even Mole, Rat must not depart from his home to follow a path that could possibly lead to still greater personal development and growth. Not only is the riverbank too felicitous to leave, but Rat is too imaginative to be permittd adventure elsewhere. In future scenes with Toad, Rat behaves, as he did on the occasion of Toad's first incarceration, just as if Rat himself had never experienced this obsessive urge to wander.

Looking back on Rat's role throughout the book, we can see that this warmhearted, generous, poetic, somewhat intellectual and modest creature is the catalyst for a network of friendships along the riverbank, a network in which he makes a place for Mole. But his central place is not only muted by Toad's colorful actions, he is virtually shoved aside and somewhat ridiculed in the last chapters, where his mock-epic compulsion for arming the warriors to the very teeth is followed by a putdown on Badger's part, when Rat attempts to correct his grammar. It is not the Riverbankers but the Undergrounders who prove themselves in the combat. By enlisting them in the external conflict against the Wild Woods, not only Toad, the misbehaving man of means, but Rat the intellectual poet, loses power. The sense of relief from the Wild Wooders is so great that the question of what the ascension of the Undergrounders might do to this felicitious space goes unasked in the supposedly happy-ever-after ending.

In Toad, whom Grahame describes as "a sanguine, self-satisfied animal," the childlike becomes childish. Toad does not merely imagine adventure, he acts out all his fantasies and, as a creature of adult means far greater than the others, can afford to do so. He becomes so much the center of the external conflict of the book and is apparently so unreflective that the notion of inner conflict and of development and growth may seem inappropriately applied to him. Indeed, viewed as an adult, he can be seen, as he is by Peter Green, as the embodiment of the manic-depressive personality, ricocheting between wild kleptomaniacal flights and utter despair.[9] Of all the characters, his creation alone, however, is firmly tied to the continuing bedtime and epistolary narrative that formed a bond between Grahame and his son.

This genesis suggests that one might view Toad slightly differently from the others—as a projection not only of those childish impulses still operative in many adults, even to pathological extremes, but also as a projection of a real child. Toad can fruitfully be seen as representative of a child struggling to control his impulses and tailor his needs to the demands of society (and as acting out in a way that can offer catharsis to a young listener).

Viewed in this way, Toad's wild departure and return not only has all the Odyssean overtones, but also takes on a circular pattern that begins when he escapes out of the window of his bedroom and ends, not with the taking of the Hall, or even the banquet at which he is not allowed to officiate. The true ending or crisis in this pattern of development takes place back in his bedroom again when he sublimates his need to display himself by playing out the banquet scene as he would have liked it to be: with himself as star in a performance of the triumphantly solipsistic ballad, "Toad's Last Little Song," with its topophilic refrain, "When the Toad—came—home!"

From the standpoint of class and of the societal ethic that Grahame preserves in this tale, Toad Hall belongs to Toad by inheritance and ought, ideally, to be his felicitous space and his true home. By participating in the cleansing, even in a lowly manner, he in some ways earns his right to return. However, no child or adult reader could be absolutely convinced of Toad's true reform (or perhaps even desire it, since it would be a dull book without his antics). His reform is dubious because, viewed as an adult rather than a child, Toad is simply the opposite of topophilic man. When he sees the motor car, he realizes its potential for movement from place to place. He rhapsodizes in a topo*phobic* vein in chapter 2: "The poetry of motion! the *real* way to travel! The *only* way to travel! Here today—in next week tomorrow! Villages skipped, towns and cities jumped—always somebody else's horizon. . . !" (*W*, 38).

Even Toad can be touched by homesickness. In prison, in response to the request of the jailer's daughter to tell her something "real" about his home, he waxes eloquent about it. His true sense of it as felicitous space is centered on the banquet hall and the exercise of his rights as host to entertain guests. He is, of course, not going to be allowed to retain this concept of his felicitous space, but is going to have his crisis in his own room—the place where middle-class children generally have theirs. Within this limited space, Toad seems to have made some real progress in self-control. He makes his bedroom felicitous space by using it himself as a place to get past the censors who want to repress his self-aggrandizing needs. This is the same bedroom in which he had been locked by his friends and, before his escape, reduced to lining up chairs and pretending he was driving a car. In the second bedroom scene, he goes voluntarily to his room to do his acting out in private, rearranging these same chairs to serve as an audience for his irrepressible song. His demure and modest (some would say disingenuous) silence at the banquet becomes possible only because he has made this somewhat shaky step toward finding a true home in his own house.

The relationship of Toad and Badger enhances this depiction of Toad as a child rather than an adult. Badger, despite rough manner-isms, is as Olympian as they come in *The Wind in the Willows;* he and Toad are at opposite poles in the need for security and the need for adventure. Badger's badgering makes security doubtfully attractive to the reader, in spite of the charm that one might find in Badger's un-derground hospitality. As a protector, Badger, unlike Pan, requires conformity to society's norms. His friendship with Toad's father brings to the fore the question of generational conflict that often pre-vails in the relationship between fathers and sons. His treatment of Toad at the end suggests that not all prodigal sons get served the fat-ted calf on their return home. Portly's reunion with his father has suggested all that is warm and welcoming about father's relationships with their sons; Badger's welcome to Toad is limited and demand-ing—the other side of the picture of the father-son experience, the side more familiar to Grahame himself.

Within its total context, Toad Hall emerges as space not entirely felicitous, for it becomes a symbol of responsibility to place that, for all its luxury, may become onerous. Rat's modest dwelling is still large enough for entertaining and seems even at the end confirmed as true felicitous space, as it was in chapter 1 where Mole first spots it as "a nice snug dwelling place . . . for an animal with few wants and fond of a bijou riverside residence, above flood level and remote from noise and dust" (*W,* 4–5).

Density of Style

A dense prose style is one that, through various stylistic devices, manages to convey more than one level of meaning and imply more than one type of audience. Like many of the classic English children's books of the late nineteenth century, *The Wind in the Willows* may be said to exhibit a "density" of style quite foreign to most modern writing for children, at least in the United States. There are probably now few American children who can understand and enjoy *The Wind in the Willows* without its being introduced to them by an interested adult whose own enthusiasm (and oral reading ability) will bring out its varied charms.

Those episodes that involve Toad are likely to be most intriguing to the young on first reading. This should come as no surprise, since Toad, in particular, was shaped to suit the child audience, and his adventures, at least in outline, come into the book almost unaltered. Indeed, a useful way of reaching an understanding of the density of style that prevails in the book is to examine the original fifteen letters still available in *First Whispers of "The Wind in the Willows,"* to see how they are at first written in that less dense style that we may consider most suitable to children. One can notice how the stylistic changes that Grahame made in enclosing the Toad incidents in his wider context seem deliberately to expand the audience to adult readers—fairly sophisticated adult readers at that—while still maintaining some contact with the child audience.

The book maintains this contact largely through the dramatic dialogue and inserted songs, which have changed little from the original letters. Even in those chapters written later, the way in which the characters speak to each other is consistently simple and close to school-boyish: full of colloquial expressions, some of them juvenile taunts and insults, rather hackneyed in its use of descriptive adjectives like "jolly" and "stupid," with a tendency toward onomatopoetic ejaculatives like "poop, poop," and an occasional memorable, but still colloquial phrase, like the famous "messing about in boats." Grahame uses no particular dialect to distinguish any of his characters from any other, but does attempt to make Badger speak gruffly and ungrammatically.

When Grahame came to write the later chapters in the book he obviously, then, made a conscious or unconscious decision to keep the dialogue at a level very accessible to children. None of the characters, for instance, though obstensibly adult, employs the courtly, but sometimes obscure language to which even pleasant Olympians in the Golden Age stories are sometimes prone (although Toad can wax rather pompous in the Wide World). The greatest change came in the manner of narration, not only in terms of expansion of details and

addition of whole scenes, but in terms of sentence structure and vocabulary—all of which move away from the general simplicity of the
epistolary narration, which, however, itself begins to expand and become more dense as the letters continue through the 1907 summer of
separation of father and son. [10]

Much of the material in the early original letters is covered in what
is known as the "paratactic" style, one variety of which is the "run-
on" sentence, common to child and unsophisticated narrators in general. In the first of the letters that Miss Stott saved, dated 10 May
1907, we read for instance that Toad "got out of the window early
one morning & went off to a town called Buggleton, & went to the
Red Lion Hotel & there he found a party that had just motored down
from London & while they were having breakfast he went into the
stable-yard & found their motor-car & went off in it without even
saying Poop-poop! And now he has vanished & everyone is looking
for him, including the police. . . ." [11]

Although parataxis has a certain effectively breathless quality, this
was certainly not the quality which Grahame was willing to retain in
chapter 6, where these incidents are expanded to some two-and-a-half
pages, forming a central but small part of the whole of the chapter,
inserted between new scenes. The transformation which this run-on
sentence has undergone includes not only expansion of detail and extended use of metaphor, but a movement toward the density that a
more complex and varied syntax conveys. The insertion of modifying
phrases, extended metaphor, and subordination of various kinds
transforms the phrase "& went to Buggleton" to the following mean-
dering discourse: "Meanwhile, Toad, gay and irresponsible, was walking briskly along the high road, some miles from home. At first he
had taken bypaths and crossed many fields, and changed his course
several times, in case of pursuit; but now, feeling by this time safe
from recapture, and the sun smiling brightly on him, and all Nature
joining in a chorus of approval to the song of self-praise that his own
heart was singing to him, he almost danced along the road in his satisfaction and conceit" (W, 118). This paragraph is followed by another—rendering one of the many self-congratulatory soliloquies that
Grahame gives to Toad—before Toad finally reaches the Red Lion.

As the letters go on, however, they do get longer and longer and
include more and more of the material that will go in the final chapters. Moreover, the narrative style, while retaining "and" as a major
connective, becomes syntactically more like the final product, so that

changes in the book form become mainly those of vocabulary, rather than of substance and syntax. Grahame's characteristic later vocabulary alterations serve two purposes: to make sentences more alliterative and to substitute literary for colloquial expressions. For instance, "Down with the Toad" in the eighth letter becomes "Down with the desperate and dangerous Toad" in chapter 10; "a bad pain in his tummy" in the seventh letter becomes "a sickening pain in his interior" in chapter 10. These are surface effects and do not necessarily increase the density of the prose which was already becoming more complex in the later letters.

This increased density of the letters themselves over the course of the summer may have two sources operative in the final version of the book as well: one, Grahame is no longer directly focusing on a child audience alone, as he might be forced to do while telling bedtime stories, and two, because he is actually writing rather than telling, he begins to compose in the written rather than the oral mode. Increased dramatic complexity toward the end of the letters, where several characters are speaking at once, points also to a written rather than a spoken story.

Certainly, when Grahame came finally to think in terms of a book and compose for it, his prose became consistently more dense, even in the dialogue. In at least one later added scene, where Toad's three friends come on their self-styled "mission of mercy" to rescue him from his motor car mania, Grahame manages to convey an extra layer of meaning through his choice of words. The language of both the narration and the dialogue in the beginning of chapter 6 is shot through with the kinds of words that missionaries and tractarians use in order to save their backsliding brethren from the fires of hell; unfavorable light is cast on the friends' outspoken wish to "convert" Toad, simply by association with such zealousness.

Parody, in general, becomes a stronger and stronger element in the style; this parody is not limited to the Homeric scenes or the extended similes, sometimes used seriously, but often as part of the *mock*-epic nature of book. The two scenes that follow Toad's theft of the motor car in chapter 6, both new to the book, are, for instance, parodic in differing ways: the courtroom scene makes mockery of local justice by distorting legal language. The scene where Toad is carried off to jail and brought struggling to the "grimmest dungeon that lay in the heart of the innermost keep'" employs language known to the nineteenth- or twentieth-century reader largely through popular approximations of "medieval" English (*W*, 124–25). These scenes are playful and largely decorative, adding little to the plot, but much to the density of the effect; their appeal seems likely to be limited, in the first case, to the adult and to the child who know something about the legal system (enough to distrust it), and, in the second case, to the adult and the child who have read much popular historical fiction (and are fond of phrases such as "Odds bodikins!").

The parodic element serves far deeper purposes in *The Wind in the Willows* than just allusion to Homer or humorous effect, or even the capture of an adult audience. This aspect of Grahame's prose would lend itself well to a much fuller application of the techniques of modern critical scrutiny, such as "deconstruction," than can be undertaken here. One might fruitfully examine such passages as the one quoted earlier, where Mole first sees Rat's home, in chapter 1. Mole first catches sight of it as "a dark hole in the bank opposite"; his musing about its probable qualities moves quickly from one level of reality to another, converting the dark hole "to a nice snug dwelling place for an animal with few wants." The imaginative transition between these two levels is not difficult for even a child to make, but here the sentence continues, still describing the "animal with few wants" but designating him as "fond of a bijou riverside residence" (*W*, 4–5). Only the sophisticated reader might make sense of, let alone find special meaning in, this last phrase. The notion of a "bijou residence," that is, a treasure of a home, comes from first the already affected language of the late nineteenth-century aesthetes, and then from its almost simultaneous debasement into real-estate advertisements; it adds a special parodic note to this description.

The passage just examined conveys its primary layer of meaning— the felicitous nature of Rat's home—at first quite straightforwardly. A reader of any age could therefore choose to ignore the end of the sentence. However, the way in which the passage toys with the notion of a hole in the riverbank being a home and then reflects on the ways in which men choose to think about their dwellings, including writing about them for the purpose of influencing others, demonstrates Grahame's complex manipulation of language and his use of stylistic devices to convey multiple layers of meaning, some of them self-reflexive and not all of them readily accessible to the child reader.

Grahame's "Coleridgean Method" of Composition

The standard reference work for the "sources" of *The Wind in the Willows* is *First Whispers of "The Wind in the Willows,"* edited by Elspeth Grahame, Kenneth Grahame's wife. The small book contains valuable material, but is limited. Not unnaturally, Elspeth Grahame's bias was to find her husband's inspiration largely within the family circle. She includes anecdotes about both a maid and then a guest overhearing Grahame's telling of a bedside story to Alastair about animals; Toad came into outside notice as early as May 1904. She relates an encounter with an actual mole in the garden: Grahame rescued it from a fight with a robin but, before he could show it to his son the next morning, it was probably killed by the housekeeper, who mistook it for a rat. Elspeth Grahame plays up Alastair's special gifts as a listener and sensivity and creativeness in general. She reprints the story of "Bertie's Escapade," which Grahame wrote in 1907 for the newspaper produced by Alastair and a young friend, as well as the letters saved by Miss Stott. However, she minimizes Constance Smedley's part in encouraging the final version of *The Wind in the Willows*. Mrs. Grahame is also rather shaky on dates; she thinks *The Headswoman* was published in 1890. While the texts that she includes are valuable, her understanding of literary sources and analogues lacks depth. Grahame's official biographer, Chalmers, is hardly more analytical.

One must go to Peter Green for an in-depth analysis of the psychological underpinnings, contemporary references, and literary sources and analogues of *The Wind in the Willows*. He finds that Grahame had a "Coleridgean method" of composition, in the process of which Grahame, like Coleridge, allowed a number of "associated motifs and fragmentary memories" to gather in the "well of the subconscious," and then to reemerge "transmuted" by the "creative imagination."[12] Green takes his terminology and method of analysis from John Livingston Lowe's *The Road to Xanadu,* the groundbreaking book Lowe devoted to tracing the sources of Coleridge's *Rime of the Ancient Mariner* and "Kubla Khan."

In this similar, but more limited analysis, Green finds Grahame to be still struggling with those contrary forces in his makeup that have been present throughout his adult life: his mid-Victorian sense of duty is in conflict with his aesthetic and intellectual leanings, which scorn the institutions the Victorians revere. In Green's eyes, Grahame's marriage upset the delicate balance that Grahame managed to achieve by the late nineties. Grahame can no longer write hopefully of a realistic solution to this conflict when he "grows up," yet he is still unable outwardly to rebel. When Grahame turns to a animal fantasy in an Arcadian setting he can project a simpler life, relatively free from restraint. Nevertheless, as Green recognizes, although Grahame has succeeded in artificially eliminating (or, as some suggest, sublimating) "the clash of sex," he has not succeeded in blanking out completely societal pressures from above, below and all about. Indeed, the strength of the book comes from the fact that Grahame is writing ambivalently about things that matter deeply to him, however lighthearted he wishes to appear.

As Grahame does so, Green finds that Grahame projects parts of himself—and to some extent of his son Alastair—into all the characters in book. But he also uses friends like Atkinson, the carefree Fowey bachelor and sailor, as one of several real life models for Rat, just as he uses Dr. Furnivall, "a compulsive but harmless exhibitionist," as one of Toad's progenitors. According to Green, Grahame's method is eclectic. Both the Thames, so much a continuing part of Grahame's life, and the Fowey rivers provide models for the riverbank. Nor are Grahame's nature descriptions or character types simply taken from his own experiences alone—literature as well as life implements his composition. Green singles out passages about the river that are very similar to those of Richard Jefferies's nature writing and points out the likeness of Rat in certain ways to an "Old Water Rat" in Oscar Wilde's story, "The Devoted Friend," published in *The Happy Prince* in 1888.

That particular likeness is a striking one. Wilde's Water Rat is introduced in this manner: "One morning the old Water-rat put his head out of his hole. He had bright beady eyes and stiff grey whiskers, and his tail was like a long bit of black indiarubber. The little ducks were swimming about in the pond . . . and their mother . . . was trying to teach them how to stand on their heads in the water."[13] This bright-eyed creature, watching the ducks "up tails all" as Rat does in the beginning of chapter 2, also seems superficially like Rat in his life-style. Wilde has him say, "I am not a family man. In fact I have never been married, and I never intend to be. Love is all very well in its way, but friendship is much higher. Indeed, I know nothing in the world that is either nobler or rarer than a devoted friendship."[14]

If one reads on further, one discovers that Wilde's Water-rat has a rather limited ideal of friendship that is tested and fails to meet the test. Nevertheless, the strong similarities as well as the even greater differences between the two water rat characters support Green's contention that Grahame uses his sources in an organic way. All of his sources—psychological conflict, life experiences of people, places, objects, and literary material—are transformed and integrated in patterns individual to Grahame himself.

The same seems true of another possible influence. The atmosphere in Dickens's *The Posthumous Papers of The Pickwick Club* (1837) seems more analogous to that prevailing in *The Wind in the Willows* than any other single book. Dickens's band of good friends and jolly bachelors—the scholarly Pickwick, the amorous Tupman, the poetic Snodgrass, and the sporting Winkle—as a group seem to maintain the particular type of relationships common to Grahame's creatures. They also, in general, enjoy a life style similarly full of the creature comforts of food and drink and, although the Pickwick group is more errant than Mole, Rat, and Badger (since they are about as wandering as Toad might like to be), the Pickwickians seem to share the same need for felicitous space. The words that Andre Maurois uses to describe Dickens's work could, with the exception of the last phrase, well be applied to *The Wind in the Willows:* "A whole picture of rural England rose up, a very eighteenth century and rural England, alive with that sort of childlike delight which the English take in simple pleasures, the enjoyment of roaring fires on the hearth, sliding in snowy weather, a good dinner, and simple, rather absurd love-affairs."[15]

Unlike Dickens, Grahame is no longer able, as he was in *The Headswoman,* lightly to satirize the relations between the sexes, so the absurd love affairs are noticeably absent in *The Wind in the Willows* except in faint suggestions in the scenes between Toad and the jailor's daughter. Yet, some of the major incidents in *Pickwick* are echoed in the later book: for instance, the trouble with a recalcitrant horse and Pickwick's imprisonment. Strong analogies can be drawn, many of which may simply mean that Grahame, in the guise of an animal novel for children, is, in addition to following a Homeric tradition, also operating in a British tradition, which combines the pastoral with the lightly picaresque. Such a conclusion would only serve to reenforce Green's demonstration that Grahame is extremely eclectic in gathering the psychic raw materials for a work that will unify all of these diverse influences and, in Lowe's terminology, "transmute" them through the exercise of an individual "creative imagination"— so that the whole becomes greater than the sum of its parts.

Modern Evaluations and Adaptations

Since the publication of Green's groundbreaking study in 1959, *The Wind in the Willows* has been subject to much scrutiny of the sort that Grahame tried to avoid when he wrote to Teddy Roosevelt about the book: "Its qualities, if any, are mostly negative—i.e.—no problems, no sex, no second meaning."[16] As Green comments, "on the internal evidence of the book itself this is . . . flagrantly untrue."[17] Green goes about gathering "circumstantial evidence" that demonstrates if not ulterior purpose on Grahame's part—which he so consistently denied—at least inadvertent portrayal of the external and internal conflicts, psychological and social, delineated in the interpretation given in this chapter.

Scholarly studies. Since Green's study, which itself was reissued in a shorter, more heavily illustrated edition in 1982, a number of dissertations and articles have taken off in many directions, on paths that Green often pointed out but did not follow. With the upsurge of academic interest in children's literature in the universities in the 1970s, *The Wind in the Willows,* like other acknowledged classics in the field, became a prime candidate for this type of analysis.

For instance, in her doctoral dissertation on "the child in pastoral myth" (1977), Phyllis Bixler Koppes asserts that Grahame succeeded through the use of literary fantasy (as he had not done in the more realistic *Golden Age* stories) in achieving a balance between child and adult roles and in creating a sense of community and cooperation.[18] In her multilevel interpretation of the book, she delineates more fully than Green how the main characters of *The Wind in the Willows* "can fit quite comfortably within the Freudian model of the human psyche: Toad is the embodiment of the unrestrained energetic force of the Id which evokes the discipline of that Super-Ego, Badger. Rat and Mole, who are in the foreground of most of Grahame's book, represent the mediating Ego."[19]

Appearing about the same time, Geraldine Poss's article describes *The Wind in the Willows* as "an epic in Arcadia," examining the nature of the transformation of the Odyssean elements within a traditional pastoral romance setting.[20] She also shows that this transformation is in the direction of eliminating women from all consideration, and she articulates the regressively antifeminist element in the book.

My own article, entitled "Toad Hall Revisited," used Bachelard to examine the search for felicitous space.[21] Perhaps in response to my

overemphasis on the expression of a need for security and on the ameliorative nature of the ending, Marion Hodge and Roderick McGillis,
in their more recent readings, both emphasize the restlessness, longing, and a virtual "divine discontent" that also exist beneath the surface of the work.[22] They and several others have pointed to the dubious nature of Toad's reformation.

The politically conservative implications of the book and its relationship to the socioeconomic trends of its time were more fully explored in 1982 by Green himself in an article entitled "The Rentier's
Rural Dream."[23] Others writing on this theme have included Julius
Zanger in "Goblins, Morlocks and Weasels: Classic Fantasy and the
Industrial Revolution," and Tony Watkins in " 'Making a Break for
the Real England': The River Bankers Revisited."[24] Watkins picks up
on the fact that shortly after 1 January 1983, when *The Wind in the
Willows* came out of copyright, the English Tourist Board began a
series of advertisements featuring Toad, Mole, or Rat "riding in a
vintage car or consulting a map on their way to a castle." The accompanying slogan read "The Real England: Make a Break for It." Watkins's article demonstrates how an Arcadian fantasy becomes part of
the sense of "national heritage" (for Americans, too!) even if Grahame's vision had to be subtly altered to include the motorcar as a
positive element.

Although Grahame would have preferred it, no serious commentator recently has talked about the book in such a fundamentalist vein
as A. A. Milne in his introduction to the 1940 Rackham illustrated
edition: "One does not argue about *The Wind in the Willows*. . . . The
book is a test of character. We can't criticize it because it is criticiz-
ing us. . . . It is a Household Book."[25] On the contrary, continued
academic interest in *The Wind in the Willows* has substantiated the
complexity of Graham's vision and its multiplicity of meanings,
rather than those "negative qualities" that Grahame claimed for it.
The book has lasting appeal precisely because adults can argue about
it and be interested enough in it to want to pass it on to their children by reading it with them.

Adaptations. Difficulties in capturing this complexity and
multiplicity have prevented neither illustrators from attempting to
picture the riverbank world nor dramatists and moviemakers from in-
vading it.

Milne, himself, protesting his inadequacy all the while, was, of
course, the first to make a play of the book, entitled *Toad of Toad*

Hall. The playwright shared a stall with Grahame and his wife when they came to see the production. The Grahames were either very polite or unfeignedly delighted with the play, as Milne described it. While Milne cut out a great deal, he was hesitant to make many other changes from the original in the parts he did retain. Such hesitancy was hardly true of Walt Disney, who, in 1949, combined Washington Irving's *Sketch Book of Geoffrey Crayon* (1819–20) and *The Wind in the Willows* in a curious amalgamation entitled "Ichabod and Mr. Toad" (Disney had previously made a film of *The Reluctant Dragon*).

Another animated version, using the voices of several renowned actors, was later made for television.[26] Perhaps the most "far-out" of dramatizations, however, was a musical produced at the Folger Theatre in the summer of 1983.[27] The latter was innovative in intriguing ways, making the weasels into "punk-rockers" dressed in black leather, and turning Mole into a brainy young female who finally wins the heart of a dreamily unresponsive Rat. Since Grahame denied social commentary and advertised his book as "free from the clash of sex," such transformations do violence to his stated intent, yet they certainly, if somewhat unsubtly, pinpoint tensions beneath the surface of the text.

Such adaptations, whether dramatically noteworthy or not, are worth considering not only to note the way in which classics become "popularized" but to determine whether such popularizations are likely to be the only way in which a book like *The Wind in the Willows,* with its difficult prose style, will reach children, particularly American children, today. One recent commentator, Harry Allard, describes *The Wind in the Willows* as "a masterpiece, elegantly layered, as in a pied Italian ice."[28] Such elegantly layered works are often an acquired taste, as *The Wind in the Willows,* even with its appeal to many basic appetites, has proved to be among modern children.

Chapter Seven

Grahame's Place in the Golden Age of Children's Literature

For many who look back on the history of children's literature in Great Britain and the United States, the period between the publication of Lewis Carroll's *Alice's Adventures in Wonderland* in 1865 and World War I is the Golden Age of children's books. Earlier considered primarily a didactic instrument and imaginatively trammeled by this role, children's literature seems in this era to exhibit the full verbal range of the imaginative faculty—from nonsense versification to metaphysical speculation. At the same time, children's books (like the adult novels of the nineteenth century) appear also to have become attuned to reality, both in the rounded depiction of character and in the expansion of content to the problems and conflicts of everyday life.

Although such categorizations are frequently misleading oversimplifications, the literature of this period did indeed shape the development of both fantastic and realistic books for children at least up until the time of World War II. Even as we approach the twenty-first century, influential children's "classics" from this period often are the basic texts in the canon for the study of children's literature in colleges and universities. Among them are *Little Women* [1868], *At the Back of the North Wind* [1871], *The Adventures of Tom Sawyer* [1876], *Treasure Island* [1883], *Heidi* [translated 1884], *Pinocchio* [translated 1899], *The Story of the Treasure Seekers* [1899], *The Wizard of Oz* [1900], *The Tale of Peter Rabbit* [1901], *Just So Stories* [1902], *The Wind in the Willows* [1908], and *The Secret Garden* [1911]. More surprisingly, perhaps, most of them are still circulating among children themselves, even if brought to their attention largely by adults.

On the basis of *The Wind in the Willows,* and sometimes *The Reluctant Dragon* and *Bertie's Escapade,* the only works of his directed at a child audience, Grahame's contribution to this Golden Age is often perceived as belonging exclusively to the realm of animal fantasy.

This is too narrow a view of his place in children's literature. *The Golden Age* and *Dream Days* were not written for children, but Grahame contributed to the development of the realistic element in children's literature in his depiction of the orphaned siblings engaged in both daydreams and imaginative play, and, more particularly, to that special branch of children's literature, the domestic or family novel. His standing must, therefore, be examined and assessed in more than one realm, although the status of *The Wind in the Willows* is clearly of prime importance.

The Animal Novel

In using animals anthropomorphically, Grahame places himself in a long storytelling tradition that extends back in time—a worldwide tradition both oral and written, not limited to stories for children. Commonly in this tradition, anthropomorphic animals appear in short fablelike tales pinpointing, often humorously, but always sharply, human foibles and failings; they also appear in longer cycles of tales, like those about Reynard the Fox and Brer Rabbit, which highlight a particular human character type—the trickster or confidence man. These cycles are related to the picaresque adventure with human protagonists and are similarly episodic in structure.

Stretching the anthropomorphic tradition. Grahame was certainly aware of this background and of the tradition in its various manifestations. His introduction to *A Hundred Fables of Aesop*, for all of its protest against man's use of animals in fables, gives its own paradoxical twist to the fable form. Grahame showed great interest in Joel Chandler Harris's *Nights with Uncle Remus* (1883), with its rendition of the South African Brer Rabbit trickster tales in Harris's notion of the black dialect spoken by his recently freed informants.[1] Grahame derives from the tradition a conscious sense of the continued attraction of humanized animals for the human audience, young and old, and a—perhaps less conscious—sense of the possibilities of eluding both internal and external censors in using animals rather than humans. In addition, harking back to an even older, pagan, tradition, in which gods manifest themselves in animal and half-animal forms, Grahame had a near mystical idea of a buried, long-lost relationship between human and animal—expressed in his *Pagan Papers* essays, "The Lost Centaur" and "Orion." This paganistic sensibility that he shares with a number of fin de siècle British writers is not only connected with Grahame's intuition of a conflictual dualism within human beings, but also leads him to a romanticized vision of a past Golden Age in which animals and human beings were able to communicate freely with each other.

In *The Reluctant Dragon,* Grahame playfully depicts such communication and at the same time manages to reverse the archetypal image of the dragon as evil, laying the groundwork for a number of "revisionist" children's stories, in which animals do not behave in ways, represent forces, or partake of characteristics that the long tradition of anthropomorphic tales has laid down for them. Although Grahame's influence would be hard to trace in the first case, both L. Frank Baum in *A New Wonderland* (1900) and E. Nesbit in *The Book of Dragons* (1900) use comic dragons.[2] Nesbit's Last Dragon, in a book by that title published in 1925, seems to be a direct descendant of Grahame's Dragon. Nesbit's tale is almost entirely revisionist in both its feminism and its pacifism. T. H. White plays with parodic elements similar to those in Grahame's story, when in *The Sword in the Stone* (1938), the first book of *The Once and Future King,* White develops the symbiotic relationship between the bumbling knight, Sir Pellinore, and the Questing Beast. Closer to their archetypal images in purport, yet as anthropomorphized and colloquialized in speech as Grahame's Dragon, are the dragons featured in Tolkien's *The Hobbit* (1938) and his *Farmer Giles of Ham* (1949).

Long experience with the fable form strongly suggests to readers elements of social satire in *The Wind in the Willows* as well. Grahame denied such, but satiric elements obviously managed to elude his internal censors. More consciously, Grahame seems to have formed Toad in the trickster mold, which fits so well with his allusion to Ulysses. Grahame also partook of the heavy reliance on dialogue in the animal cycle tales: characters there spend much time talking to each other and manipulating each other through verbal cleverness. Grahame's mysticism with regard to animals, which is more satisfactorily embodied in pagan than in Christian forms, must have had much to do with placing "The Piper at the Gates of Dawn" at the center of *The Wind in the Willows.*

Grahame's use of the ancient tradition of animal stories, enhanced by a pagan sensibility, does not, however, totally account for the special quality of this book, a quality that distinguishes it from its literary predecessors like *Alice's Adventures in Wonderland* and *Wood Magic*

(1881), with their young human protagonists. Strangely, considering Grahame's failure to turn *The Golden Age* and *Dream Days* into novels, the key to the difference is the book's unity in creating a world in which humans are peripheral. Considered with regard to form rather than substance, what seems to distinguish *The Wind in the Willows* is that Grahame manages to incorporate all of these traditional anthropomorphic elements into a new structure, which one might call the animal novel. *The Wind in the Willows* is a book of fair length, with well-developed animal protagonists, who participate in a similarly well-developed plot, built on conflict, both internal and external, to some resolution of those conflicts. Grahame's ability to develop and sustain this novel form, without the use of human protagonists, must indeed rest on the vitality and strength in his own imagination of those human characteristics with which Toad, Mole, Rat, and Badger are endowed, as well as on Grahame's ability to project them living their daily lives in an anthropomorphic manner and a natural setting that fascinated him. Moreover, he is able to embody in both the lifestyle and the landscape not only the tensions but the satisfactions of his own life.

Writing for the child and artist within.   This view of *The Wind in the Willows* as the first animal novel emphasizes some aspects of the work that are particularly associated with its continued popularity among adults, after they have supposedly outgrown it (although children too are attracted by adult self-indulgence). This view of *The Wind in the Willows* is also not entirely a traditional one, even though it certainly follows from Peter Green's examination of the relationship between Grahame's life and works. Such a view of *The Wind in the Willows* takes less account of the inspiration of Alastair on the work than of the Grahames' move back to Kenneth Grahame's childhood home, Cookham Dene. It finds few strong traces of the bedtime story in the completed work and notes that even the letters written to Grahame's son change in style, becoming denser and more dramatic over the course of the summer of 1907.

Such a view, therefore, makes one consider again what C. S. Lewis has to say about Grahame in "On Three Ways of Writing for Children," where Lewis claims that his own Narnia tales were written with no children in mind, but only because a children's story was "the best art-form for something [he had] to say."[3] Lewis finds his own approach to be in contrast with the way in which *The Wind in the Willows,* and also *Alice's Adventures in Wonderland* were written.

Carroll and Grahame, according to Lewis, wrote for a particular child and, presumably, therefore, were meeting different, more external demands perhaps less deeply centered in self than those of Lewis. As others have demonstrated for Carroll, and as Green seems to demonstrate for Grahame, Lewis's dictum may be a misdirection of critical attention. Despite its original source in Alastair's bedtime stories and letters to Alastair, when completed, *The Wind in the Willows*—like *The Reluctant Dragon,* which came before Alastair's existence, and even *Bertie's Escapade,* written for Alastair's newspaper—seems a response to internal demands, as much as to a child listener or reader. Grahame, like Carroll before him and many another writer for children, writes as much for the child and the artist within as for the child without.

When an adult who has many sophisticated literary tools at his disposal, as Grahame does, writes for both an external and internal audience, he or she is likely to produce a multilayered work in which the fictional characters, events, and settings are both an expression of, and a defense against, deep-seated needs and emotions. In *The Wind in the Willows,* Grahame's great achievement was to sustain, for a previously unequaled length of time, a tale in which the characters are all animals, permeating it with an emotional and sensual resonance of great importance for both its unity and its continued appeal. In doing so, Grahame uses animals in the whole range of ways in which human beings have drawn on animals in either tale-telling or ritual: to express their own humanity in all its aspects from the ridiculous to the sublime, and to draw into themselves those powers that they perceive animals to have and they themselves to have lost.

As already noted, Grahame's ability to use animals in this way ranges widely from the humor of satire to the mysticism of pagan totemism. His own contribution to this range is his ability to dwell on the particular details of a Pickwickian life-style that express deep-seated desires common to both adults and children. Who else has depicted quite so graphically the oral satisfactions of good food as well as good talk? Grahame's menus are justly famous for both their gourmet and gourmand qualities—not only the catalog in chapter 1 of all the wonderful foods in Rat's picnic basket (which echoes the midnight supper in *Bertie's Escapade*), but the whole range of fully realized delights, from the buttered toast that the jailkeeper's daughter brings Toad in prison—"cut thick, very brown on both sides, with butter running through the holes of it"—to the sophisticated al fresco offer-

ing of Rat to the Sea Rat—"a yard of long French bread, a sausage
out of which the garlic sang, some cheese which lay down and cried,
and a long-necked straw-covered flask containing bottled sunshine
shed and garnered on far Southern slopes" (*W*, 145, 181).

Most of all, however, Grahame projects onto his animal characters
his own conflicts between a need for security and a need for adventure, expressing them for the most part in those simple terms he
deems appropriate to "wise, small things" and thus making his conflicts accessible to children. At the same time, Grahame's adult longing to partake of an animal simplicity—a simplicity that he perceives
adult human beings lack—comes through to his adult readers. Some
of the latter have remarked that *The Wind in the Willows* is a book
full of longing. The characters are always responding to "calls" that
are an externalization of such longing. Perhaps the greatest longing
that comes through at the adult level is the longing to be free from
longing. This negative freedom is one that no human child is likely
to desire, but which Grahame at some level is able to project onto
most of his animal characters (with the possible exception of Toad) by
the end of the book.

The Grahame tradition.   Such characteristics are not easily
transferable. Even Grahame himself could not write a sequel. No
wonder that most of Grahame's followers in children's literature, except insofar as they share some of Grahame's deep-seated longings,
derive from Grahame's animal novel only some of the elements of
childlike charm, gentlemanly comaraderie, lively dialogue, and, in
some cases, orality, that are pervasive in *The Wind in the Willows*. A.
A. Milne, in his tales of Winnie the Pooh and Christopher Robin
(1926–28), seems to skim these elements off the surface of Grahame's
book, cutting off their deep roots in the process of projecting them
onto animals that are one layer farther from reality since Milne's creatures are stuffed nursery toys rather than river and wood dwellers. In
The Hobbit, Tolkien's Hobbit characters, small humanoids with hairy
feet, maintain a life-style not unsimilar to that of Grahame's protagonists and are as deeply rooted in tradition and human need as Grahame's creations.[4] But the Hobbits experience different tensions in a
fantasy world where grand external conflict is envisioned and adventure is rewarded rather than punished.

C. S. Lewis adopts the gentlemanly bachelor life-style for several of
his adult characters, like Mr. Tumnus, the Faun, in *The Lion, the
Witch and the Wardrobe* (1950). (Tumnus, incidentally, like Pan in

The Wind in the Willows, has been purged of his goatish qualities.) Lewis too shows himself to be in some ways also intrigued by the pleasures of eating and drinking among friends. For instance, in chapter 7 of this book Lewis describes in some detail the simple fish and bread supper that the children of this book share with the anthropomorphized Mr. and Mrs. Beaver. But Lewis imbues his work with Christian symbolism; this meal can be read not only as the fish and loaves distributed by Christ, but as a Last Supper because during it Edmund, the Judas figure, slips away to betray the savior, who appears in the form of Aslan the Lion. Attempts to read a similar Christian symbolism into Grahame's scene of Pan, with Pan as a protective Christ figure, have never really worked, for Grahame is truly attracted to paganism and his writing is nonallegorical, while Lewis manipulates paganism allegorically for Christian purposes. Similarly, good food and good drink among good gentleman friends have a value for Grahame in themselves—a value that none of those fantasists who follow him convey.

One must go to a children's book that is not an animal novel to see the influence of Grahame's pagan mysticism. Published in 1911, three years after *The Wind in the Willows,* Francis Hodgson Burnett's *The Secret Garden* shows this influence. Burnett creates in the rural youngster, Dickon, a benevolent Pan figure, gathering the animals to him with music and helping Mary and Colin to effect rebirth through nature. More directly, she echoes the Piper at the Gates of Dawn scene in her own twenty-first chapter. There Burnett describes moments of intense but elusive epiphany in communion with nature, moments when "one is quite sure one is going to live forever and ever and ever": "One knows it sometimes when one gets up at the *tender solemn dawn-time,*" or in the woods at sunset "and the mysterious deep gold stillness slanting through and under the branches seems to be saying slowly again and again *something one cannot quite hear,* however much one tries." She continues: "sometimes *the sound of far-off music* makes it true."[5]

There are strong contrasts between the two books, however. Competing with Dickon, the Pan figure in Burnett's book, are two powerful maternal influences, Mrs. Sowerby, Dickon's and Martha's mother, and Colin's dead mother, who first planted the Secret Garden. Burnett's restorative Nature is clearly Mother Nature, even when she brings about a reconciliation between Colin and his father. The contrast between the two books in this regard reminds us again

of how embedded in *The Wind in the Willows* is the paternal ideal and
at what a deep level women are excluded there.

Reflecting more closely the paternal emphasis in *The Wind in the
Willows,* as well as its anthropomorphic use of animals, are T. H.
White's four books about Arthur, gathered into the volume known as
The Once and Future King (1958), a book that, like Grahame's, is today
perhaps better known among adults than children. White's anguish
about World War II and his concern about the aggressiveness and
hostility in himself and others embues this book with some of the
subterranean tensions one senses in *The Wind in the Willows*. Scattered
through the first book of the tetralogy are the experiences of becoming a member of one or another species of animal, experiences that
Merlin, as Arthur's tutor, uses to educate young "Wart," as he is
called. These animals include a scholarly badger and an impudent
lower-class hedgehog, as well as an arrogant upper-class falcon, all of
whom reflect the British class consciousness and partake of various
British life-styles that White projects with a gusto similar to that of
Grahame. Showing most clearly Grahame's influence is a fifth book,
originally intended as a conclusion for the tetralogy but unpublished
until 1977.[6] In *The Book of Merlyn,* as it is called, not only does the
nearly defeated Arthur visit with Merlin a committee of animals, who
meet in the well-appointed badger set, with its own extensive library,
but Arthur, walking toward dawn with the rather grubby and ver-
minous Hedgehog, experiences an epiphany that in its insight is different from that of Rat and Mole in the Piper at the Gates of Dawn,
but belongs to a similar topos.

In recent times, Richard Adams's *Watership Down* (1972), certainly
an animal novel, has attracted both juvenile and adult audiences. Adams (who lived for some time on the same Berkshire Downs as Grahame) creates a tribal rabbit society that reflects an attraction to a
more primitive life-style than the one Grahame projects, however;
thus his characters seem less anthropomorphized than do Grahame's.
In the introduction to a reissue of Richard Jefferies's *Wood Magic,* Adams indicates the influence on his work of this earlier animal fantasy,
featuring a young human protagonist, Bevis, who witnesses and par-
ticipates in a power struggle of the animals and birds against both a
ravaging weasel and a tyrant magpie. Although Adams, like Grahame, has eliminated the human protagonists to create an animal
novel, his concerns and his anthropomorphic projections, like Jefferies's, are somewhat different from Grahame's.

Many Americans seem to have been enough intrigued by some version of *The Wind in the Willows* (perhaps Milne's or Disney's) to have named restaurants and homes after Toad Hall, but Grahame's novel, possibly because of the pervasiveness of a characteristically British lifestyle, seems to have influenced mainly British writers of children's literature. Randall Jarrell's *The Bat-Poet* (1963), however, combines in its anthropomorphic title character the immortal longings of Rat with the humility of Mole; Jarrell's *The Animal Family* (1965) seems quite different in quality, yet does reflect, in its collection of diverse species into a family group, Grahame's own longings for communion among the species. Also, both E. B. White and Robert O'Brien might be considered to work in the Grahame tradition of the animal novel. Like *The Wind in the Willows*, *Charlotte's Web* (1952), in its barnyard center, and *Mrs. Frisby and the Rats of NIMH* (1971) in its entirety, create animal worlds and relationships full of human complexity. These relationships and worlds express concerns that are of great moment for the authors themselves; both books embed them as firmly as Grahame's does in the lives and adventures of the characters; they attest to the continued vitality of the animal novel.

The Family Novel

If one might describe the animal novel as alive and well in children's literature in the late twentieth century, one might similarly describe the family novel as still thriving even in the convoluted forms of "the new realism" or "problem novel." Grahame's association with the family novel and his place in the tradition is not well established. For instance, a recent study of "the family story of the 1960's" does not mention Grahame's *The Golden Age* or *Dream Days* in its historical survey of precursors.[7]

Certainly such an association was the opposite of what Roger Lancelyn Green had in mind when he insisted, despite his own well-remembered distaste for *The Golden Age* as a child, that the book is "one of the most important landmarks in children's literature." Green goes on to say that the child had earlier been pictured as an "undeveloped adult" who must be forced into "life's full flowering" and that Grahame for the first time "presented childhood as a thing in itself . . . a good thing, a joyous thing . . . a precious experience to be recaptured out of the past and presented truly and lovingly for its own sake."[8] Like many who now read *The Golden Age* and *Dream Days,* Green seems captivated not only by the nostalgia but perhaps by the relatively static, nondevelopmental quality of the work. He also makes much of its distance from the long and—it should be pointed out essentially female—tradition of the domestic children's stories with, in the late eighteenth and early nineteenth centuries, clearly stated didactic aims. These might be best exemplified by Mrs. Barbauld's *Hymns in Prose for Children* (1781), Thomas Day's *Sandford and Merton* (1783–89), Maria Edgeworth's *Early Lessons* and *Moral Tales* (1801), and Mrs. Sherwood's *The History of the Fairchild Family* (1818–47).

R. L. Green apparently perceives that didactic tradition as dominant up to Grahame's time, even though other recent critics discern clear movement toward more realistic and less didactic depictions of family life in the American works of Louisa May Alcott and the British children's books of Catherine Sinclair, Mrs. Ewing, Mrs. Molesworth, and even the religiously motivated Charlotte Yonge, depicter of enormous Victorian families. Grahame no doubt did see himself as in reaction to any and all of that "cursed Barbauld crew" of authors (as Charles Lamb called the early female writers for children).[9] In the last story of *The Golden Age* he certainly alludes disparagingly to the "profligate curates and harrowing death beds" of Charlotte Yonge (*D,* 257). This does not mean, however, that Grahame's concept of the child as a total human being—interesting in his or her own right and operating within a complex of familial relationships, not only with parental figures (many previous writers had depicted orphans) but with siblings—was born in a vacuum. Victorian novelists in general were depicting childhood both in its complexity and in an adversarial position to Olympian adulthood: Dickens's Pip of *Great Expectations,* Charlotte Brontë's Jane Eyre, and George Eliot's Maggie Tulliver of *The Mill on the Floss* are fully projected child figures. Grahame was certainly familiar with all of them.

The whole child.   Grahame was surely if vaguely remembering disaffected Maggie Tulliver's visit to the Gypsies when he cites this example of the human urge to get back to "the Garden" in his essay "Orion": "This is it that sends the little girl footing it after the gypsy's van, oblivious of lessons, puddings, the embrace maternal, the paternal smack, naught save the faint, far bugle summons to the pre-historic little savage that thrills and answers in the tingling blood of her" (*P*, 106). Eliot, like Grahame, saw the child as a complex creature of imaginative ingenuity, capable of suffering great pain, yet she too looks back on childhood as a kind of golden age.

This same passage from "Orion" depicts "the small boy [thrust] out under the naked heavens, to enact a sorry and shivering Crusoe on an islet in the duck-pond" (*P*, 106–7). It too takes us back to some of Grahame's predecessors in the realistic depiction of childhood, this time in children's literature. Of all the writers who came before, Grahame would perhaps have most readily acknowledged his debt to Mark Twain. He knew *Huckleberry Finn* (1885) well; among other qualities, its river imagery was no doubt attractive.[10] *Tom Sawyer* (1876) may or may not have been available to Grahame in his adolescence, while Jefferies's *Bevis: The Story of a Boy* (1882), with its similar boyish island adventure, did not appear until Grahame was already a young man. Nevertheless, both depict boyhood in ways analogous to Grahame's depiction. Those who remember *Tom Sawyer* from childhood reading are likely to emphasize the adventure story aspect of the book, but those who reread the book as adults will recognize Twain's pervasive social satire of Olympian (i.e., adult) follies. Also apparent to such readers will be the complexity of Tom's character: his capacity for melancholic depression and remorseful brooding, his ability to immerse himself in imaginative games based on literary heroes; his romantic vulnerability to young girls; his ability to lead and manipulate others. Bevis is a similarly complex young boy. To some extent Edward, Harold, and more particularly the narrator in *Dream Days* are cast in the same mold as Tom and Bevis, and even though Grahame does not involve his characters in sustained adventures, he maintains in them Tom's and Bevis's adversarial but somewhat ambivalent relationship to Olympian authority.

Both Tom and Bevis, like Grahame's young boys, are still bound by domestic ties. They are in contrast to Stevenson's young boys who actually have adventures at sea. Stevenson's *Treasure Island* (1883) and *Kidnapped* (1886) also were published during Grahame's young manhood, and in the essay "The Long Odds" (1895) Grahame remarks that "it ought not to be necessary to put forward preface or apology for finding oneself immersed in *Treasure Island* for about the twentieth time."[11] Despite this interest in reading adventure stories, Grahame does not write them. The sea adventures that Stevenson's characters act out become a part of Grahame's characters' solitary daydreams and group imaginative play, contributing to a much more complex portrayal of the boy character than Stevenson's.

Thus, while Grahame's depiction of the domestic scene obliquely comments on the depiction of the family in domestic children's novels of the past, even their indulgence in daydreams and imaginative games (when the heroes of adventure stories act) mark Grahame's characters as belonging to the same domestic rather than adventure novel tradition. Grahame's elaboration of the imaginative aspects of child life is, however, his great contribution to this type of literature for children.

"**The Nesbit Tradition.**"   Just as Grahame's depiction of the domestic scene comments on his predecessors in the family novel, E. Nesbit comments on Grahame's depiction at the same time as she is clearly influenced by its portrayal of children engaged in daydream and imaginative play. Echoes of Grahame's *The Golden Age* can be discerned in the composition and activities of the semiorphaned family of six Bastable children—*The Story of the Treasure Seekers* (1899), *The Wouldbegoods* (1901), and *The New Treasure Seekers* (1904)—as well as those of the temporarily semiorphaned family of three in *The Railway Children* (1906). Yet one should also note that Nesbit, in the best way of followers of a tradition, comments critically on her very sources, both explicitly and implicitly.

Nesbit knew *The Golden Age* well. In chapter 5 of *The Wouldbegoods,* Alice, one of the two Bastable twins, receives a book for her birthday; Oswald Bastable, the weakly disguised boy narrator, comments: "it was *The Golden Age,* and is A1 except where it gets mixed up with grown-up nonsense."[12] What Oswald (and, to some extent, Nesbit herself) might discern as grown-up nonsense remains to be discovered in Nesbit's own handling of a participating narrator, and in incidents such as the finding of a "princess" and the children's relationship with an Indian uncle in *The Story of the Treasure Seekers.*

Scholars find Nesbit's use of this participatory narrator to be mainly derived from Dickens's child narrators in *A Holiday Romance* in their parodic use of language and self-consciousness about the art of writing itself. To some extent, however, the use of Oswald also follows and comments upon Grahame's nameless retrospective adult narrator as well. Oswald, who at first also tries to remain nameless (but fails miserably to hide his own identity), displays all the self-absorption and considerable blindness of Grahame's narrator as a young boy, without the benefit of the older narrator's hindsight. Yet without this retrospection comes also none of the adult nostalgia or patronizing tone. Instead, the identification of the reader with the Bastable children is strengthened through the child narrator, while Oswald's perceptions are tested by the other children themselves, especially by the girl characters and sensitive Noel, the poet, whom Oswald, perhaps more in the bullying pattern of Grahame's Edward than of Grahame's narrator, considers to be practically a girl.

In this area of the relations between the sexes, Nesbit, who always denied any feminist leanings and came out against women's suffrage, nevertheless provides challenges to the relatively mild antifeminism that appears unchallenged in *The Golden Age* and *Dream Days*. In Nesbit's works, exclusions of the girls from activities in which the boys participate are bitterly grieved. Boys' interest in girls as romantic or sexual objects capable of betrayal in this area are not a part of Nesbit's portrayal. Noel's finding of a child princess and subsequent "marriage" in *The Story of the Treasure Seekers* is devoid of the sexual innuendos that permeate Grahame's narrator's voyeuristic experience with a princess in *The Golden Age* and sea idyll with the rescued princess in *Dream Days*. Harold's comparison of Selina and her girl friends to chattering rabbits and Edward's scornful expansion of this comparison in "What They Talked About" is picked up consciously or unconsciously by Nesbit. In *The Railway Children,* this same comparison becomes an integral part of the young boy Peter's education in not teasing his sisters.

Like the Golden Age children, both the Bastable children and the Railway children are capable of getting into trouble with grown-ups, and not all adults are equally responsive to them. The ones who are, both male and female, frequently resemble Grahame's good Olympians in their ability to join in childlike imaginative play. But in Nesbit's work, children and grown-ups are not generally in adversarial position to each other. She emphasizes children's power rather than powerlessness, while Grahame does so only in *The Reluctant Dragon*. The Bastable children's Indian uncle does not become a distant giver of coins and buyer-off of children as does "The White Washed Uncle," for the children persuade him not only to participate in their games but to give money to their father for investment. The children in *The Railway Children* manage not only to save a train and a Russian refugee, but to get their father out of jail. Olympian vulnerability is clear in Nesbit's work—as, to a greater extent than normally recognized, it is in Grahame's stories—but the Golden Age children are given the capacity neither to perceive nor to act upon this vulnerability in order to increase their own power.[13] In contrast, Nesbit's children, within the realistic story context, are unbelievably powerful. Grahame more accurately reflects reality: relegating his only really powerful child figure to the fairy-tale land of *The Reluctant Dragon* and recording visions of *adult* power in his narrator's youthful daydreams.

Whatever may be these differences between Grahame's and Nesbit's conceptions of childhood, Grahame's *Golden Age* children through their influence on Nesbit are swept, willy-nilly, into the mainstream of twentieth-century children's literature in the wake of what has been called "The Nesbit Tradition."[14]

Conclusion

The spring of Grahame's personal inspiration went dry, or at least sought other, underground, channels after welling up so copiously in *The Golden Age,* the *Dream Days* stories, and *The Wind in the Willows.* Yet the last alone was enough to earn Grahame a permanent place both in the canon of children's books and in a broader British heritage, literary and popular, in which the figures of Toad, Rat, Mole, and Badger have taken on a legendary aura. Ironically, at the turn of the century Grahame himself was commemorating an earlier imaginary Golden Age. But for our generation his animal characters have become symbols of an imaginary Golden Age of Great Britain that supposedly existed as short a time ago as just prior to World War I. *The Wind in the Willows* characters still represent an idyllic vision that goes against all dictates of historical reality. This fact suggests the force of the underground flow that Grahame tapped for his own inspiration and the corresponding pressure of the popular urge to return to, or nostalgically imagine, an Arcadian past.

Notes and References

Chapter One

1. Kenneth Grahame, in a 1908 letter to Charles Scribner's Sons, his American publisher, quoted by Charles Scribner IV in the preface to *The Wind in the Willows* (1908; reprint, New York: Charles Scribner's Sons, 1965); hereafter cited in the text as *W*.

2. According to Constance Smedley, Grahame told her, "I can remember everything I felt then, the part of my brain I used from four till about seven can never have altered. . . . After that time, I don't remember anything particularly" (quoted in Peter Green, *Kenneth Grahame, 1859–1932* [London: John Murray, 1959], 17–18).

3. "Oxford Through a Boy's Eyes," *Country Life,* 3 December 1932; reprinted in *Kenneth Grahame: Life, Letters and Unpublished Works,* by Patrick Chalmers, (London: Methuen & Co., 1933), 17–26.

4. "The Good and Bad Effects of Rivalry." *St. Edward's School Chronicle,* no. 5 (October 1873).

5. See "A Funeral," never published in Grahame's lifetime, probably written ca. 1890, reprinted in Chalmers, *Grahame,* 28–31. It describes early disappointments and death of past hopes in a personified but not specific fashion.

6. Green, *Grahame,* 68.

7. Ibid., 201.

8. Ibid., 77–78.

9. Chalmers, *Grahame,* 44.

10. Green, *Grahame,* 100.

11. "By a Northern Furrow," *St. James's Gazette,* 26 December 1888—reprinted in Chalmers, *Grahame,* 189–94; "A Bohemian in Exile," *St. James's Gazette,* 27 September 1890—reprinted in *Pagan Papers* (London: Elkin Mathews & John Lane, 1893), 73–83. *Pagan Papers* is hereafter cited in the text as *P*.

12. See Jerome Hamilton Buckley, *William Ernest Henley: A Study in the Counterdecadence of the "Nineties"* (Princeton: Princeton University Press, 1945), and Joseph M. Flora, *William Ernest Henley* (New York: Twayne Publishers, 1970).

13. Chalmers, *Grahame,* 48.

14. Green, *Grahame,* 201–2.

15. Flora, *Henley,* 57.

16. Green, *Grahame,* 134.

17. Ibid., 93, 169.

18. Chalmers, *Grahame*, 50–51.

19. "A Parable (Overheard and Communicated by Our Own Cat)," *St. James's Gazette*, 19 November 1890; reprinted in Green, *Grahame*, 109–10.

20. Green, *Grahame*, 75, 244.

21. Ibid., 207–16.

22. Ibid., 226.

23. Ibid., 289–90.

24. Eleanor Graham, *Kenneth Grahame* (London: Bodley Head Press, 1963), 43.

25. Scribner IV, preface to *The Wind in the Willows*.

26. Green, *Grahame*, 1.

27. Chalmers, *Grahame*, 213.

28. "The Fellow That Goes Alone," *St. Edward's School Chronicle* 12 (July 1913):270–71; reprinted in Green, *Grahame*, 4–6.

29. Green, *Grahame*, 329.

30. "Ideals," *Fortnightly Review*, December 1922; reprinted in Chalmers, *Grahame*, 258–73.

31. Ernest H. Shepard, "Illustrating *The Wind in the Willows*," introduction to *The Wind in the Willows* (1965).

32. Eleanor Graham, *Grahame*, 60.

33. "Sanger and His Times," preface to *Seventy Years a Showman*, by George Sanger (1925; reprint, New York: E. P. Dutton, 1926), 5–29.

34. "A Dark Star," *Cornhill* 74 (June 1933): 649–67.

35. Chalmers, *Grahame*, 215–16.

36. "Sanger and His Times," xx–xxi.

Chapter Two

1. Vergil, *Georgics*, 2.1.493.

2. Ibid., 1.1.485.

3. "A Funeral," in Chalmers, *Grahame*, 28–31.

4. Sir Thomas Browne, *Religio Medici* (ca. 1642), ed. J. J. DeNoriden (Cambridge: Cambridge University Press, 1953), 24.

5. "By a Northern Furrow," in Chalmers, *Grahame*, 189–94.

6. Ibid., 190–91.

7. Ibid., 192.

8. Ibid., 193–94.

9. Ibid., 194.

10. According to the *OED*, when the word Bohemian does not refer to a citizen of Bohemia, "the transferred senses are taken from the French, in which *boheme, bohemian*, have been applied to the gipsies . . . because they were thought to come from Bohemia . . . thence, in modern French, the word has been transferred to 'vagabond, adventurer, person of irregular life habits,' a sense introduced into English by Thackeray."

11. I am thinking here of Bronte's depiction of Jane Eyre, Dickens's

young Pip in *Great Expectations,* George Eliot's Young Maggie and Tom in *The Mill on the Floss,* and Twain's Tom Sawyer and Huckleberry Finn. Richard Jefferies's adolescent Bevis might also qualify in this regard, as well as certain aspects of the younger Bevis in *Wood Magic.*

12. For example, see description of William Sharp's *Pagan Review,* in Green, *Grahame,* 138–39.

13. Ibid., 117.

14. Ibid., 137.

15. The contrast between the technological and the natural is similar to that found in nineteenth-century American writing. See Leo Marx, *The Machine in the Garden: Technology and the Pastoral Ideal in America* (New York: Oxford University Press, 1964).

16. Green, *Grahame,* 122–23, compares and contrasts Grahame with both Freud and D. H. Lawrence in this regard.

17. Hugh Holman, *A Handbook to Literature,* 3d ed. (New York: Odyssey Press, 1972), 205.

18. Ded-Larry Pebworth, "Wandering in the America of Truth: *Pseudodoxia Epidemica* and the Essay Tradition," in *Approaches to Sir Thomas Browne,* ed. C. A. Patrides (Columbia: University of Missouri Press, 1982), 172.

19. Chalmers, *Grahame,* 51.

20. Robert Louis Stevenson, "An Apology for Idleness," in *Virginibus Puerisque and Other Papers* (1881; reprint, New York: Standard Classics Publishing Co., 1930), 60–71.

21. Ibid., 63.

22. Ibid., 65.

23. These lines seem to echo in a suggestive way Psalm 24, "The earth is the Lord's and the fulness thereof; the world and they that dwell therein," as well as the end of the Lord's Prayer: "For thine is the kingdom, and the power, and the glory."

24. Stevenson, *Virginibus,* 135.

25. Ibid., 144–48.

26. Green, *Grahame,* 127.

27. Richard Jefferies, *The Story of My Heart* (1883; reprint, London: Eyre & Spottiswoode, 1949), 25.

28. Ibid., 28.

29. Ibid., 25.

30. Green sees Grahame's ending as a welcome and witty introduction of "deliberate bathos to lower the emotional temperature" (*Grahame,* 128).

31. Eleanor Graham, *Grahame,* 26.

32. Green, *Grahame,* 116.

33. Ibid., 119.

34. Green interprets the train ride in "Romance of the Rail" as referring to the Grahame children's trip to Scotland to spend a last year with their father (*Grahame,* 29).

35. Chalmers, *Grahame*, 209–10.

36. This interpretation seems even more viable if one reads parts of this fragment omitted by Chalmers, which include a debate between "Ego" and "sub-conscious Ego" about whether to get an M.A. without either financial help or approval from relatives. See Green, *Grahame*, 54, 356.

37. "The Iniquity of Oblivion," *Yellow Book*, October 1895; reprinted in Chalmers, *Grahame*, 129–36.

38. Ibid., 130.

39. Ibid., 131.

40. Ibid., 133.

41. Green insists that Grahame was "not a wistful anarchist who lacked the courage of his convictions; the division, the battle was in himself" (*Grahame*, 54). This seems all the more reason for Grahame to wish for a solution *beyond* his control.

42. "The Long Odds," *Yellow Book*, July 1895; reprinted in Chalmers, *Grahame*, 75–83.

43. Ibid., 83.

44. In a fragment from his ledger, Grahame depicts the South as a tropical island where "new life and strength flowed in with every moment of warmth and peace." He contrasts it to the "northern island, arena of strife and all the crowd of petty vexations" (Chalmers, *Grahame*, 37).

45. Ibid., 129. An analogy between the beachcomber in "The Long Odds" and the Seafaring Rat, with Grahame as Ratty, seems even more apt, especially since Chalmers seems to see Grahame as Mole, rather than Ratty. But then, perhaps, he was all three.

46. Green, *Grahame*, 4–6.

47. Ibid., 5.

48. Ibid., 6.

49. Ibid., 5.

50. Chalmers, *Grahame*, 258–73.

51. Ibid., 272.

52. "Sanger and His Times," 5.

53. Ibid., 28.

54. Chalmers, *Grahame*, 18–26.

55. Ibid., 19.

56. Ibid., 26.

57. Ibid., 286–310.

Chapter Three

1. See Elspeth Grahame, introduction to *First Whispers of "The Wind in the Willows,"* by Kenneth Grahame (Philadelphia: J. P. Lippincott, 1944).

2. "The Triton's Conch," *National Observer*, 23 December 1893; reprinted in Chalmers, *Grahame*, 173–76.

3. "An Old Master," *National Observer*, 28 April 1894; reprinted in Chalmers, *Grahame*, 249–52.

4. "The Inner Ear," *Yellow Book*, October 1895; reprinted in Chalmers, *Grahame*, 69–73.

5. Ibid., 70.

6. Ibid., 71.

7. Ibid., 72.

8. Introduction to P.J. Billinghurst's *A Hundred Fables of Aesop*, trans. Sir Robert L'Estrange (London: John Lane, 1899), i–iv.

9. Ibid., iv.

10. Ibid., v.

11. In his piece, "The Barn Door," *National Observer*, 28 October 1897 (reprinted in Chalmers, *Grahame*, 202–4), Grahame takes a much more realistic look at animal existence. The narrator observes decaying carcasses nailed to a barn door and acknowledges the cruel mortality humans share with animals.

12. "The Invention of Fairyland," *Academy*, 18 December 1897; reprinted at the end of *Dream Days* (London: John Lane, 1899), 3–8.

13. Ibid., 4.

14. Ibid.

15. Green, *Grahame*, 135.

16. *The Headswoman*, (London: John Lane, Bodley Head, 1899); hereafter cited as *H* in the text.

17. Green makes all these suggestions for interpretation, in *Grahame*, 158–59.

18. This is an apt allusion, for Alice squelches Bill-the-Lizard (whom Freudian critics see as having phallic associations) not once but twice in the course of her adventures in Wonderland: first when he attempts to come down the White Rabbit's chimney and again when he is in the jury box.

19. Green, *Grahame*, 158.

20. Introduction to *A Hundred Fables*, vi–viii.

21. Ibid., vi.

22. Ibid., vii.

23. Ibid., viii.

24. "The Fabric of the Fairy Tale," *Daily Mail*, 16 December 1899; reprinted at the end of *Dream Days*, 11–15.

25. Ibid., 15.

26. Introduction to *A Hundred Fables*, xi.

27. "The Reluctant Dragon," in *Dream Days* (1898; reprint, New York: Garland Publishing Co., 1976), 149–202; this edition hereafter cited in the text as *D*.

28. Green, *Grahame*, 182–83.

29. *Bertie's Escapade* (Philadelphia: J. B. Lippincott, 1949); hereafter cited in the text as *B*.

30. Green, *Grahame*, 249–50.

Chapter Four

1. Quoted in Green, *Grahame*, 160.
2. Stevenson, "Child's Play," in *Virginibus Puerisque*, 132.
3. *The Golden Age* (1895; reprint, New York: Avon Books, 1975), 3; hereafter cited in the text as *G*.
4. Roger Lancelyn Green, in *Tellers of Tales, Children's Books and Their Authors from 1800–1968*, rev. ed. (London: Kaye & Ward, 1969), 204–5, comments on this patronizing tone when he describes what he disliked about *The Golden Age* when he was a child. See also Laura Krugman Ray, "Kenneth Grahame and the Literature of Childhood," *English Literature in Transition* 20 (1977):3–12.
5. Peter Green sees this passage as characteristic of the influence of Sir Thomas Browne's humanistic morality on Grahame's writing (*Grahame*, 188).
6. Stevenson, "Child's Play," 126.
7. Again confirming the composite nature of this family, Green finds that Grahame derived a number of Harold's fanciful notions not from his own childhood experience but from observation of children of friends, particularly one young boy named Anthony Feiling (*Grahame*, 20).
8. Stevenson, "Child's Play," 127.
9. Green points to "The Secret Drawer" as revealing Grahame's method of composition, which was to transpose items from his adult life, like the antique bureau that was one of Grahame's early antique purchases, to this childhood scene (*Grahame*, 88).
10. Ibid., 88.
11. Ibid., 161. Green cites a contemporaneous review by Professor Scully that objects not only to the "precocious poetic raptures" of the boy narrator in *The Golden Age*, but also to his reading into the scene of "Sawdust and Sin" "a significance that could only have occurred to an experienced adult."
12. Stevenson, "Child's Play," 123.

Chapter Five

1. Green notes that Grahame is referring here to medievallike folios from William Morris's Kelmscott Press (*Grahame*, 262).
2. Grahame's vision of the city seems to be made up of those glimpses of walled towns afforded by medieval painting and by his visits to Italy, his experience of Oxford (a town modeled on such medieval cities), and an image of "The New Jerusalem" taken from the biblical Revelations that was part of the prevailing notion of "Utopia" in the literature of Grahame's time.
3. A similar princess is depicted in an 1896 essay, "Saturnia Regna" (Chalmers, *Grahame*, 103–9).

4. Green describes "The Reluctant Dragon" as "the reconciliation of Grahame's conflicting selves" (*Grahame,* 182).

5. Ibid., 185.

Chapter Six

1. Green, *Grahame,* 256–59; see also Chalmers, *Grahame,* 123–29.

2. *First Whispers,* 51–94.

3. Quoted in Green, *Grahame,* 226.

4. Gaston Bachelard, *The Poetics of Space,* trans. Maria Jolas (New York: Orion, 1964).

5. Quoted in Green, 17–18.

6. See both Lucy Waddey, "Home in Children's Fiction: Three Patterns," *Children's Literature Quarterly* 8 (Spring 1983):13–14, and Christopher Clausen, "Home and Away in Children's Fiction," *Children's Literature* 10 (1982):141–52, for interesting discussions of characters' relationships to their homes in children's literature in general and in *The Wind in the Willows* in particular.

7. The entire letter is reprinted in Chalmers, *Grahame,* 62–63.

8. All of the following emphasize Mole's importance: Richard Matthew Skoket, "Functions of Voice in Children's Literature" (Ph.D. diss., Harvard University School of Education, 1971); Peter Hunt, "Necessary Misreadings: Directions in Narrative Theory for Children's Literature." *Studies in the Literary Imagination* 18 (Fall 1985):116; Humphrey Carpenter, *Secret Gardens: A Study of the Golden Age in Children's Literature* (Boston: Houghton Mifflin, 1985); Neil Philip, "Kenneth Grahame's *The Wind in the Willows:* A Companionable Vitality," in *Touchstones: Reflections on the Best of Children's Literature* (West Lafayette, Ind.: ChLA Pub., 1985), 96–105.

9. Green, *Grahame,* 282–84.

10. An article by Elizabeth A. Cripps, "Kenneth Grahame: Children's Author?" *Children's Literature in Education* 12 (Spring 1981):15–20, first suggested to me the fruitfulness of examining differences in syntax between the original letters and the book.

11. *First Whispers,* 51.

12. Green quotes from John Livingston Lowes, *The Road to Xanadu* (Boston: Houghton Mifflin, 1927 [pp. 427–28]): "The notion that the creative imagination, especially in its highest exercise, has little or nothing to do with facts is one of the *pseudodoxia epidemica* which die hard. For the imagination never operates in a vacuum. Its stuff is always a fact of some order, somehow experienced; its product is that fact transmuted" (*Grahame,* 239).

13. Quoted by Green, *Grahame,* 280–81.

14. Ibid., 281.

15. Quoted by Clifton Fadiman in the introduction to Charles Dick-

ens, *The Posthumous Papers of the Pickwick Club* (1836–37; reprint, New York: Simon & Schuster, 1949), xviii–xix.

16. Quoted by Green, *Grahame*, 274.

17. Ibid.

18. Phyllis Bixler Koppes (Phyllis Bixler), "The Child in Pastoral Myth: A Study in Rousseau and Wordsworth, Children's Literature and Literary Fantasy" (Ph.D. diss., University of Kansas, 1977).

19. Ibid., 313.

20. Geraldine D. Poss (Geraldine DeLuca), "An Epic in Arcadia: The Pastoral World of *The Wind in the Willows*," *Children's Literature* 4 (1975):80–90.

21. Lois R. Kuznets, "Toad Hall Revisited," *Children's Literature* 7 (1978):115–28.

22. Marion Hodge, in a paper delivered at the meeting of the Philological Society of the Carolinas, March 1984, and Roderick McGillis, "Utopian Hopes: Criticism Beyond Itself," *Children's Literature Association Quarterly* 9, no. 4 (Winter 1984–85):184–86. Michael Steig, "At the Back of *The Wind in the Willows:* An Experiment in Biographical and Autobiographical Interpretation," *Victorian Studies* 24 (1981):303–23, also emphasizes this ambiguity.

23. Peter Green, "The Rentier's Rural Dream," *Times Literary Supplement*, 26 November 1982, 1299–1301.

24. Julius Zanger, "Goblins, Morlocks and Weasels: Classic Fantasy and the Industrial Revolution," *Children's Literature in Education* 8 (1977):154–62; Tony Watkins, " 'Making a Break for the Real England': The River-Bankers Revisited," *Children's Literature Quarterly* 9 (Spring 1984):34–35.

25. A. A. Milne in the introduction to *The Wind in the Willows* (New York: Heritage Press, 1940), x.

26. *The Wind in the Willows*, Rankin/Bass production, Vestron Video. With Charles Nelson Reilly as Toad, Roddy McDowell as Rat, Jose Ferrer as Badger, and Eddie Bracken as Mole.

27. The Folger production, with a book by Jane Iredale, was reviewed in "Toad & Mole & Rat—Oh My!, 'The Wind in the Willows' Blows into the Folger," *Washington Post*, 8 August 1983, C3–4.

28. Harry Allard, " 'The Wind in the Willows': 75th Birthday," *Parents' Choice* 6 (Autumn 1983):15.

Chapter Seven

1. Green, *Grahame*, 61–62.

2. See Ruth Berman, "Victorian Dragons: The Reluctant Brood," *Children's Literature in Education* 15 (1984):220–33, for a fuller discussion of the dragon tradition.

3. C. S. Lewis, "On Three Ways of Writing for Children" (1959); reprinted in *Only Connect,* ed. Sheila Egoff, G. T. Stubbs, and L. F. Ashley (New York: Oxford University Press, 1969), 208.

4. See Lois Kuznets, "Tolkien and the Rhetoric of Childhood," in *Tolkien: New Critical Perspectives,* ed. Neil Isaacs and Rose Zimbardo (Knoxville: University of Tennessee Press, 1981), 150–62.

5. Francis Hodgson Burnett, *The Secret Garden* (1911; reprint, Philadelphia: J. B. Lippincott Co., 1962), 213–14; my italics. Jerome Griswold suggested to me the likenesses between this passage and the Piper at the Gates of Dawn chapter.

6. T. H. White, *The Book of Merlyn* (Austin: University of Texas Press, 1977).

7. Anne W. Ellis, *The Family Story in the 1960's* (Hamden, Conn.: Archon Books, 1970).

8. R. L. Green, *Tellers of Tales,* 204–5.

9. Charles Lamb to Coleridge, 23 October 1802, in *Letters of Charles Lamb,* ed. Alfred Ainger (New York: MacMillan and Co., Ltd., 1904) 1: 237–38.

10. Green, *Grahame,* 368–69.

11. "The Long Odds," in Chalmers, *Grahame,* 75.

12. Edith Nesbit, *The Wouldbegoods* (1901; reprinted in *The Bastable Children* [New York: Junior Literary Guild, 1929]), 89. Those stories in *The Golden Age* that seem to be echoed in *The Story of the Treasure Seekers* were published not only in periodicals prior to the publication of *Pagan Papers,* but also were among those that appeared at the end of the first edition of *Pagan Papers* of 1893, so they had been available to Nesbit long before *The Story of the Treasure Seekers.*

13. Phyllis Bixler Koppes's distinction between "Georgic" works that emphasize the redemptive power of children and "Bucolic" works that separate the worlds of adults and children seems particularly apt here in characterizing the distinction between Nesbit and Grahame. See "The Child in Pastoral Myth: A Study of Rousseau and Wordsworth, Children's Literature and Literary Fantasy" (Ph.D. diss., University of Kansas, 1977).

14. See Marcus Crouch, *The Nesbit Tradition: The Children's Novel in England, 1945–70.* (1971; reprint, Totowa, N.J.: Rowman & Littlefield, 1972).

Selected Bibliography

PRIMARY SOURCES

Most of Grahame's essays and stories first appeared in periodicals. Periodical publication is listed only when material did not appear in book form during Grahame's lifetime. When it was not possible to view first editions, information was taken from the bibliography in Peter Green's *Kenneth Grahame, 1859–1932*. No poems are cited here.

1. Novels
The Wind in the Willows. London: Methuen & Co., 1908. New York: Charles Scribner's Sons, 1965. With a preface by Charles Scribner IV (1953) and Ernest H. Shepard.

2. Collections of Short Stories
Dream Days. London: John Lane, Bodley Head, 1898. New York: Garland Publishing, Inc., 1976 (facsimile of 1902 edition). Includes "The Reluctant Dragon."
The Golden Age. London: John Lane, 1895. New York: Avon Books, 1975.

3. Collections of Essays and Miscellaneous Pieces
First Whispers of "The Wind in the Willows." Edited by Elspeth Grahame. Philadelphia: J. B. Lippincott, 1944. Includes letters to Alastair, "Bertie's Escapade."
Pagan Papers. London: Elkin Mathews & John Lane, 1893.
Paths to the River Bank: The Origins of The Wind in the Willows, From the Writings of Kenneth Grahame. Introduction by Peter Haining. London: Souvenir Press, 1983.

4. Tales
"Bertie's Escapade." In *Bertie's Escapade*. Philadelphia: J. B. Lippincott Co., 1949. First printed in Chalmers, 154–60.
The Headswoman. Bodley Booklets, no. 5. London: John Lane, 1898.

5. Introductions and Prefaces
Billinghurst, P. J. *A Hundred Fables of Aesop*, i–xv. Translated by Sir Roger L'Estrange. London: John Lane, 1899.

The Cambridge Book of Poetry for Children. Edited by Kenneth Grahame, xii–xv. Cambridge: Cambridge University Press, 1916.

Field, Eugene. *Lullaby-Land, Songs of Childhood*, 7–13. London: John Lane, 1898.

Sanger, George. *Seventy Years a Showman*, 5–29. New York: E. P. Dutton, 1926.

6. Works in Periodicals

"The Barn Door." *National Observer*, 28 October 1893. Reprinted in Chalmers, *Grahame*, 202–4 (see below).

"By a Northern Furrow." *St. James's Gazette*, 26 December 1888. Reprinted in Chalmers, 189–94.

"Concerning Ghosts." *National Observer*, 5 November 1892. Reprinted in Chalmers, 196–99.

"A Dark Star." *Cornhill* 74 (June 1933):649–67. Reprinted in Chalmers, 286–310.

"The Fabric of the Fairy Tale." *Daily Mail*, 16 December 1899, 4. Reprinted at the end of *The Golden Age* (London: John Lane, Bodley Head, 1902); partly reprinted in Chalmers, 59–61.

"The Fellow That Goes Alone." *St. Edward's Chronicle* 12, no. 321 (July 1913):270–71. Reprinted in Green, 4–6.

"The Good and Bad Effects of Rivalry." *St. James's Gazette* 5 (October 1873).

"Ideals." *Fortnightly Review*, December 1922. Reprinted in Chalmers, 258–73.

"The Iniquity of Oblivion." *Yellow Book*, October 1895, 192–202. Reprinted in Chalmers, 129–36.

"The Inner Ear." *Yellow Book*, April 1895, 73–76. Reprinted in Chalmers, 69–73.

"The Invention of Fairyland." *Academy*, 18 December 1897, 542. Reprinted at the end of *The Golden Age* (1902); partly reprinted in Chalmers, 59–61.

"Long Odds." *Yellow Book*, July 1985, 78–86. Reprinted in Chalmers, 75–83.

"An Old Master." *National Observer*, 24 March 1894. Reprinted in Chalmers, 249–52.

"Oxford Through a Boy's Eyes." *Country Life* (3 December 1932). Reprinted in Chalmers, 17–26.

"A Parable (Overheard and Communicated by Our Own Cat)." *St. James's Gazette*, 19 November 1890. Reprinted in Green, 109–10.

"Pastels." *National Observer*, 17 February 1894. Reprinted in Chalmers, 52–54.

"Saturnia Regna." *New Review* 14, no. 82 (March 1896). Reprinted in Chalmers, 103–9.

"The Triton's Conch." *National Observer,* 23 December 1893. Reprinted in Chalmers, 173–76.

SECONDARY SOURCES

1. Biographies

Chalmers, Patrick. *Kenneth Grahame, Life, Letters and Unpublished Work.* London: Methuen & Co., Ltd., 1933. For years the only easily available source of certain periodical pieces (some of which are now also available in *Paths to the Riverbank*), this is an "official" biography, published only a year after Grahame's death.

Graham, Eleanor. *Kenneth Grahame.* London: Bodley Head, Ltd., 1963. A short biography of Grahame that summarizes available material.

Green, Peter. *Beyond the Wild Woods: The World of Kenneth Grahame, Author of the Wind in the Willows.* 1982. Reprint. New York: Facts on File, 1983. An abridged version of Green's earlier biography. Provides no new material but many new photographs of the important places in Grahame's life and works.

—————. *Kenneth Grahame 1859–1932: A Study of his Life, Work and Times.* London: John Murray, 1959. Green did not have available to him certain items available to Chalmers, including the bank ledger of early writings, but he used many letters and documents left by Elspeth Grahame. Demonstrates that Grahame was an "extremely subtle and complex" man, who "crystallized in his life and writing, many profoundly important changes which affected English society towards the close of the nineteenth century" (1–2).

2. Critical Studies

Berman, Ruth. "Victorian Dragons: the Reluctant Brood." *Children's Literature in Education* 14, no. 4 (Winter 1984):220–33. In examining the dragon motif in children's literature, finds that Grahame's "The Reluctant Dragon" was instrumental in freeing the dragon from its satanic identifications. Interprets Grahame's dragon as a symbol of benign Nature.

Carpenter, Humphrey. *Secret Gardens: A Study of the Golden Age of Children's Literature.* Boston: Houghton Mifflin Co., 1985. Examines the lives and works of major British writers for children from Kingsley through Milne. Considers Grahame in a number of contexts throughout; in the chapter on *The Wind in the Willows* argues that each of the major characters stands for one level of poetic inspiration.

Clausen, Christopher. "Home and Away in Children's Literature." *Chil-*

dren's Literature 10 (1982):141–51. Proposes that one good way to determine whether or not a book is for children is its attitude toward home as a positive or negative place and finds *The Wind in the Willows,* in contrast to *Huckleberry Finn,* a children's book because of its positive attitude toward home.

Cornwall, Charles. "From the Self to the Shire: Studies in Victorian Fantasy." Ph.D. dissertation University of Virginia, 1971. In examining the works of MacDonald, Carroll, and Wilde, finds *The Wind in the Willows* to depict the necessity for compromise in the everyday world.

Cripps, Elizabeth. "Kenneth Grahame: Children's Author?" *Children's Literature in Education* 12 (Spring 1981):15–23. Uses the idea of the implied reader to discover why Grahame's *Dream Days* and his *The Reluctant Dragon* give such different evidence of being taken out of the library by children. Also analyses some of the stylistic differences between Grahame's letters to his son and the final version of *The Wind in the Willows.*

Green, Roger Lancelyn. *Tellers of Tales: Children's Books and Their Authors from 1800 to 1968.* Rev. ed. London: Kaye & Ward, Ltd., 1969. Concentrates largely on influences and trends, pairs Grahame with Nesbit and discusses the impact of *The Golden Age* and *Dream Days* on the depiction of the child and then pairs Grahame with Milne and discusses the animal fantasy.

Hunt, Peter. "Necessary Misreadings: Directions in Narrative Theory for Children's Literature." *Studies in the Literary Imagination* 18, no. 2 (Fall 1985):107–21. Argues that children and adults read with a different sense of the "grammar" of the text. Uses *The Wind in the Willows* as an example to demonstrate some possible grammars.

Koppes, Phyllis Bixler. "The Child in Pastoral Myth: A Study of Rousseau and Wordsworth, Children's Literature and Literary Fantasy." Ph.D. dissertation, University of Kansas, 1977. Distinguishes between a Georgic ideal in the literary depiction of children (emphasizing the child's ability to redeem the adult community) and a bucolic one (emphasizing the child's world as completely separate from the adults'). Finds *The Golden Age* representive of the bucolic, but *The Wind in the Willows* a mixture.

Kuznets, Lois. "Toad Hall Revisited." *Children's Literature* 7 (1977):115–28. Examines *The Wind in the Willows* in light of Gaston Bachelard's *The Poetics of Space* and his concept of topophilia (love of place). Finds both the structure of the book and its development of character to be based on a search for felicitous space.

Lowe, Elizabeth Cochran. "Kenneth Grahame and the Beast Tale." Ph.D. dissertation, New York University, 1976. Finds Grahame's adoption of the nineteenth-century romantic notion of the mystical bond between human and animal to be in contrast to both medieval and Freudian views of the relationship of human and animal.

McGillis, Roderick. "Utopian Hopes: Criticism Beyond Itself." *Children's Literature Association Quarterly* 9, no. 4 (Winter 1984–85):184–86. Argues that the ambiguity of *The Wind in the Willows* with regard to both domesticity and society allows critics to read it in radically varying ways.

Philip, Neil. "Kenneth Grahame's *The Wind in the Willows:* A Companionable Vitality." In *Touchstones: Reflections on the Best in Children's Literature,* 96–105. West Lafayette, Ind.: Children's Literature Association Publications, 1985. Argues for the continued relevance of the book for its "paean to the simple, uncluttered pleasures of friendship" (105).

Poss, Geraldine D. (Geraldine DeLuca). "An Epic in Arcadia, the Pastoral World of *The Wind in the Willows.*" *Children's Literature* 4 (1975):80–90. Traces the Arcadian elements "both positive and negative" in *The Golden Age* and *Dream Days* that led Grahame to "fashion the sweet epic in Arcadia." Argues that while heroism, heterosexual love, and death were handled, if ambivalently, in the earlier stories, they are virtually banished from this novel.

Ray, Laura Krugman. "Kenneth Grahame and the Literature of Childhood." *English Literature in Translation* 20, no. 1 (1977):3–12. Traces the influence of both Wordsworth and Dickens on Grahame's *The Golden Age* and argues that Grahame undercuts their ideas of the imagination and humanity of the child and reduces their visions to a "gentle recollection of what it once meant to be a child" (12).

Robson, William W. "On *The Wind in the Willows.*" *Hebrew University Studies in Literature.* 9, no. 1 (Spring 1981):76–106. A rereading of the novel, emphasizing literary predecessors such as Jerome's *Three Men in a Boat,* stressing the paternalism represented by Badger and suggesting that, while politically conservative, the novel yet presents a attractive image of Utopia.

Steig, Michael. "At the Back of *The Wind in the Willows:* An Experiment in Biographical and Autobiographical Interpretation." *Victorian Studies* 24 (1981):303–23. A reader-response approach emphasizing the book's ambiguity and the buried sexual implications of several passages.

Waddey, Lucy. "Home in Children's Fiction, Three Patterns." *Children's Literature Association Quarterly* 8 (Spring 1983):13–14. Claims that children's attitudes toward home correspond to three patterns reflected in literature: Odyssean (in which the protagonist feels free to explore and return home); Oedipal (in which the home is the center of development); and Promethean (in which the protagonist can create his/her own home). Finds *The Wind in the Willows* to represent all three patterns although the prevailing pattern is Odyssean.

Index

PR 4727 .K88 1987

Kuznets, Lois R.

Kenneth Grahame

PR 4727 .K88 1987

Kuznets, Lois R.

Kenneth Grahame

MERCYHURST COLLEGE
HAMMERMILL LIBRARY
ERIE, PA 16546

APR 13 1988